TONY WHITE'S
ANIMATOR'S NOTEBOOK

TONY WHITE'S
ANIMATOR'S NOTEBOOK

Personal Observations on the Principles of Movement

Tony White

ELSEVIER

Amsterdam • Boston • Heidelberg • London • New York
Oxford • Paris • San Diego • San Francisco • Singapore
Sydney • Tokyo

Focal Press is an imprint of Elsevier

Focal
Press

Focal Press is an imprint of Elsevier

225 Wyman Street, Waltham, MA 02451, USA

The Boulevard, Langford Lane, Kidlington, Oxford, OX5 1GB, UK

Library of Congress Cataloging-in-Publication Data

White, Tony, 1947-

Tony White's animator's notebook : personal observations on the principles of movement / Tony White.

p. cm.

ISBN 978-0-240-81307-3 (pbk.)

1. Animation (Cinematography) I. Title.

TR897.7.W495 2011

777'.7—dc23

2011020156

British Library Cataloguing-in-Publication Data

A catalogue record for this book is available from the British Library.

ISBN: 978-0-240-81307-3

For information on all Focal Press publications
visit our website at *www.elsevierdirect.com*

12 13 14 15 16   5 4 3 2 1

Printed in China

Typeset by: diacriTech, India

Contents

Contents

Contents

Introduction

Imagine you have rummaged through the drawers of a dusty old studio animation desk and found inside a rare personal notebook that had in it all the core secrets of movement. Imagine if all those core secrets told you everything you'll ever need to know to become a master animator yourself. Imagine that these notes were clearly written down, illustrated, and easy to understand—as if the author of the notebook wrote them down as he learned those key secrets from his own teacher. That is what I hope you'll find when you open the pages of this book!

It has to be said that I have a passion for teaching animation—traditional or digital! In every book I've written I tried to consistently improve the ways I teach the core underlying principles and process of animated movement. More recently I decided to put my collection of personal notebooks into individual, downloadable e-tutorials that teach specific principles of movement in the best and most comprehensive ways I can. Consequently 12 separate e-tutorials now exist via Focal Press online, so that if anyone wants to learn just about basic walks, runs, jumps, anticipation, flexibility, and so on, he or she can download that particular individual tutorial at the click of a mouse, day or night, anywhere around the world. It then occurred to me that not everyone has easy access to the Internet or is keen to purchase products online, so I got to thinking that perhaps I should provide a printed cover version of my notebooks, too. This is it, new and improved and focused entirely on the printed word.

Some of the material in this book will certainly be found my other books. But I believe I have now found a way to explain it better, with added information and illustrations to make this particular learning experience unique—perhaps my best ever. I hope that each chapter in this book offers perfect foundational textbook material for faculty and students involved in the teaching and learning of animation. I also hope that it provides the core material for my own personal dream—an online atelier-style studio/academy that teaches and celebrates the traditional art form of hand-drawn animated movement. Of course, only you can decide if I have indeed achieved my best teaching approach to date. If nothing else, I hope you'll find the process of learning from my notebook as enjoyable as it was for me when discovering, compiling, and refining all the material myself. I guess the proof of this particular pudding will appear through the results you'll get from following my advice.

Many of the illustrations found here are those I had used previously, although some have been revised. Some illustrations have been replaced, and some are brand new. Yet all have been pretty much drawn freshly for the purposes of this book, so there is a new and consistent design theme running throughout wherever possible.

The companion website (www.animators notebook.com) material consists entirely of pencil animation and other tests I have produced to demonstrate core principles for my previous books or master classes, as well as miscellaneous clips from commercials or films I have made. I particularly hope you enjoy viewing this film as much as I enjoyed animating it for you. Although very simple in style and format, it actually uses all the principles I will explain in this book, proving that they can work in any style, whether that be 3D, stop-frame, or any other forms of contemporary animation.

Lastly, I am presuming that you are reading this book because you want to learn animation, or you are considering enrolling in an animation school program, or you want to supplement the education you are currently receiving. If so, I have included a three-part appendix on the companion website that might be of help to you. The first part of the appendix contains a shortened version of a privately published book (*Jumping Through Hoops: The Animation Job*

Coach; ISBN 970-0-557-78618-3; www.animbooks.org) about getting a job in the animation industry that I wrote for my students (who are always looking to land a job in this field).

The second part of the appendix contains my more recent thoughts on the state of the mainstream educational system in the West right now as it pertains to art and animation teaching. In the last part of the appendix, to underline my own qualifications for writing this book, I have included my latest personal resume, including a list of awards won, so you can see where I'm coming from and what I've achieved in my career so far.

I wish you "good animating," one and all!

Tony White

http://blog.animaticus.com

www.tonywhiteanimation.com

This book includes a companion website (www.animatorsnotebook .com) with animation examples, a three-part appendix, and more. Whenever you see the Web icon in the book, the website has more to offer, like an animated example of a particular movement described in the book's text.

Acknowledgments

I wish to offer a big thanks to everyone involved in the creation of this book, from Laura, Anais, and all the other folks at Focal Press, to Saille who did stellar work in helping me write the text and then helping me color and ink all the accompanying illustrations. I'd also like to thank all my teaching colleagues over the years who have taught me so much I didn't previously know, despite my 30+ years in the animation industry. I truly hope I've honored all these fine mentors with a book that will be of significant value to every student and professional in our wonderful animation world.

Dedication

To all those who have held a pencil—or will hold a pencil—and dream of seeing what they created come alive with verve, movement, and storytelling wonder!

chapter 1

The Principles and Process of Animation

Before you can tackle animation in any serious way, you need to understand the process and principles involved. The actual "process" of animation (i.e., the way the animator actually approaches the creation of scene) is hardly ever mentioned in literature on the subject, but it is extremely important, especially if character animation is your goal.

This chapter remedies this lack of information by explaining both the process and the principles of animation right from the get-go. Reading this part of my notebook will give you a foundation of method and information at your fingertips before you attempt the actual nitty-gritty of character animation in any serious way.

But first, let's briefly review how we got to this moment in time with the finest art form known to humankind: animation!

Animation's History in a Nutshell

The first animation was achieved by drawing the images directly onto film. This process involved every image on every frame of film being drawn slightly differently from the preceding one, like an old-fashioned paper flipbook.

This process of apparent movement was preceded by such fairground novelty devices as the Thaumotrope and the Practascope. However, it was not until Emil Cohl first drew images directly onto film that animation as we know it today—with direction, action, and story—was invented and captured the public's imagination.

As time went by, a greater emphasis was placed on larger-scale drawings, initiated on paper, which were filmed and edited into short films. This gave both artists and filmmakers greater control over the subject matter, which meant that more finesse and complexity could be added to the action.

Typical of this era was the work of the great Winsor McCay, who drew incredibly complicated and intricate pen-and-ink drawings onto cards that were successively aligned and filmed afterward.

However, it was only when the animator's peg bar was invented that a precisely registered process allowed for drawings to be consistently and universally created by a team of artists, using a key and "in-between" system, as defined in the early Fleischer Brothers' cartoons, soon to be followed by those of the great Walt Disney.

OUR FOUNDER

Disney was responsible for moving the drawn cartoon tradition into entirely new areas of expression, in which a greater reality of characterization and innovative storytelling was developed to incredible degrees of innovation. Films such as *Snow White*, *Pinocchio*, *Fantasia*, and *Bambi* defined this amazing era, now often referred to as animation's Golden Age.

Even today, with the amazing digital technology that is at the fingertips of every aspiring animator, we still use the same core principles of movement defined by keys, breakdowns, and in-betweens. As a result, any instruction that applies to the process and principles of animated movement is equally valid for every form of animation that is being attempted. Even the finest animators of the fabulous Pixar studio still pretty much adhere to the same production process that was used all those years ago by fabulous traditional 2D animators at the once great Disney studio.

The Process of Animation

The first question we must address is, how does a good character animator approach the creation of a scene within a production? There are, of course, as many approaches to the animation process as there are animators attempting it—and each animator evolves his or her own methods and procedures. However, what follows is a widely acknowledged generic approach that can apply to all animation formats, even though here we deal with the two principal forms of animation: traditional 2D animation and computer-based 3D animation.

The 2D Animation Process

Traditional 2D animation is no longer at the forefront of animation entertainment, but many passionate traditional animators still prefer the handcrafted, organic feel it offers when it's executed well. For example, the recent *Spirited Away* movie, by Hayou Miyazaki, has to be considered one of the finest animated films ever made. Sylvan Chomet's *The Illusionist* is another superbly crafted traditionally animated film. Certainly traditional animators at the top of their game still have a great deal to teach their more contemporary 3D counterparts, and much of its creative potential has yet to be realized, despite the infinite number of diverse films that have been produced traditionally over the decades.

What follows is the finest traditional animation process that I've personally found most valuable when approaching effective character animation. A modern student of traditional animated filmmaking will do well to follow the principles outlined here, even if they are later modified to suit that animator's own particular preferences.

1. **Understand what you need to achieve.** This means that with whatever form of animation being attempted, the animator first must fully understand the story, the emotion, the motivation, the continuity (in other words, the scene with the scenes around it), and of course, the character acting needs for any particular scene. This can either be dictated by the director (in larger productions) or by the animators themselves on shorter, more personal films. Whatever the length or style of film being considered, however, it is a fundamental requirement of the process that the animators fully understand what they are seeking to achieve with each scene from the get-go.

2. **Key-pose thumbnails.** To assist in the animators' thinking process, it is highly
desirable that they first produce a series of dynamic thumbnail key-pose positions
for each character, expressing the kinds of dynamic key-pose gestures they have
in mind for the action. These need not be perfectly crafted drawings, just freeform
representations of the kinds of ideas that the animators feel best communicate what
they are trying to achieve. However, in producing these thumbnails, the animators
should not stop with the first ideas they think of or draw. They should push and push
their visual pose ideas till something really gels in their mind. It is very often the case
that the first thing thought of is not the best thing ultimately, so always push yourself
at this decisive stage. When this goal is ultimately achieved, however, shoot your
thumbnails in sequence as a rough-pose animatic.

(CONCEPT ART - STILL UNDER DEVELOPMENT)

3. **Reference video footage.** It is very desirable that you find video footage of the action you are attempting, or even film yourself doing that same action in a number of ways. As with invaluable life drawing sessions, observing and recording real life is much superior to relying on memory, imagination, or assumption alone to make your final gesture statements. So, wherever possible, reference either live or filmed footage to give you greater insights into the kinds of key-pose gestures and elements of movement that you need to attempt.

Important note:

Never use footage as rotoscope or motion capture material only; this will only create dead and unconvincing animation, however economically desirable or time-consuming this option might appear at the outset. On the other hand, adjusted motion capture material after the event, achieved by an experienced professional animator, can raise the level of the final animated output through this technique, although the time taken to do this properly will probably be longer than if you had attempted to animate it from scratch in the first place!

4. **Rough-pose animatic.** With all your rough poses thumbed out, it is necessary to shoot them sequentially in a way that approximates the scene action you have in mind. Although there will be some inconsistencies with time and drawing-to-drawing scale in doing this, it will at least give you a general feel as to how your scene is shaping up and the effectiveness of the key poses you are using. If modification is needed, make the necessary changes and repeat until your rough-pose animatic works as you imagine it should in your mind's eye.

5. **Final key poses.** When you're satisfied that the shape and flow of your key drawings are basically working, you can begin to draw your final key poses on regular punched animation paper. This will effectively set down final markers as to how your action will be analyzed and expressed as well as how your gestures will define the anticipated action. Even though you might well be satisfied with the thumbnail key poses you have created before, remember that this stage is where it counts. So adjust, extend, and even change your key positions here if necessary, no matter what you believed was sufficient before. Remember that exceptional animation

comes from exceptional and defining keys, not just good in-betweening. Thus the more time and effort you place in getting your key-pose gestures right, the more that effort will pay you back in the long run. (Don't forget the value of "flipping" your key frames as you create them so you can get a feel for the flow of the action as you go along.) This advice applies to computer-graphics (CG) animation as much as it does traditional 2D animation, so a strong eye and drawing ability for all animators are always advised.

6. **Key-pose animatic.** With your final key poses successfully created, shoot another animatic using these drawings instead of your thumbnail drawings. On this occasion, though, start to pay more attention to the drawings' placement and timing. Even now you don't exactly want to lock yourself down to precise timings, but you do want to make a valiant stab at it. So shoot each key pose for the number of frames you imagine it will need to get to the next key-pose frame, and do this throughout the entire scene. (Note: You are not putting in in-betweens at this stage. However, a pose test animatic will give you a strong indication that your keys are well drawn and well placed and will confirm that your action sequence is working as fluidly as possible.) Adjust your key-pose drawings and reshoot as necessary.

7. **Breakdown drawings.** At this stage I personally prefer to add all my breakdown drawings (i.e., the first in-betweens created between two keys) before going any further. Breakdown drawings are not literal in-betweens for much of the time. More often than not they are carefully located midpositions that are positioned to enable the timing, emphasis, or arc movement required. This means that they are not necessarily precisely in the middle of the two keys being linked together, and all the elements within the drawing are not necessarily equally centered. Therefore, place a great deal of attention on your breakdown drawings because they will control the way your action will best unfold from key to key. (Note: I deal with the issue of breakdown and in-between variations in a later notebook tutorial.) Flip your drawings as you go along so that you can assess the flow and consistency of action, and then shoot your revised key-pose animatic with the breakdown drawings included. Adjust and reshoot as necessary.

8. **Rough in-betweens.** Now that you have your keys and breakdowns completed, drop in the very rough in-betweens as you envisage them. Timing is always a difficult thing for an animator, especially a novice one, to assess. So it might be trial and error before you arrive at a decision about how many in-betweens will be needed to link each key and where you will place them. As a trial-and-error process, it really will help if you just sketch these in very roughly (but accurately) for now. This will save you a huge amount of work later if you need to make changes after your first pencil test is viewed.

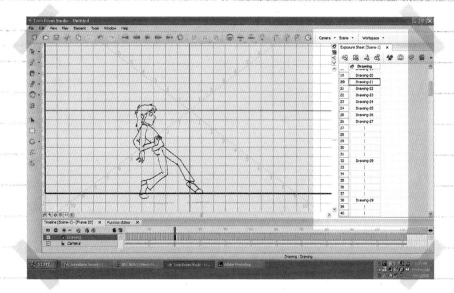

9. **First pencil test.** With roughly drawn in-betweens finally in place, you should shoot a first pencil test of everything. Most traditional animators work on *two's* (one drawing for every two frames), at least to review the initial animated action. However, once these are seen and approved, they might decide to add *one's* later; these are usually reserved for complex, fast-moving action or drawings that appear very large on the screen.

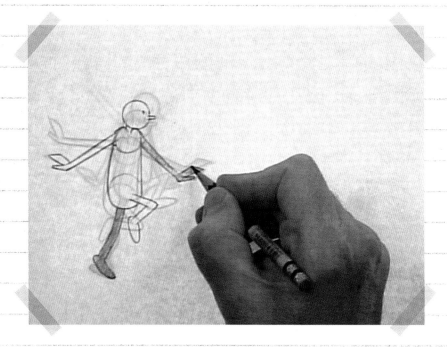

10. **Rough in-between adjustments.** Adjust and reshoot with new in-betweens as necessary. When you are happy with your final pencil test, you can move on to the final stage of the process: your cleaned-up animation.

11. **Clean-up.** The clean-up stage is where all the rough and reworked drawings of your animation are carefully redrawn, neatly and accurately, to reflect the original design of the character you are working with. On large-scale productions this task is usually handled by a dedicated clean-up department. The main challenge a major production faces is consistency of character drawing and proportions from animator to animator, which is why the clean-up stage is essential to overcome all these challenges. Whether it involves part of a large team effort or simply an animator cleaning up his or her own work, the clean-up process invariably involves tackling the keys and breakdown drawings first. At this stage it is advised that these cleaned-up drawings be shot as a pose test. This tests for any errors or inconsistencies that may appear in the clean-up drawings. If all is well, then the rest of the in-betweens can be cleaned up accordingly.

12. **Final pencil test.** The last stage of the 2D process is for the cleaned-up animation drawings to be shot as a final pencil test for the director or animator to sign off on. In the old days of cell animation this used to be done on film in a camera. Nowadays, however, this is usually done by shooting the drawings with a digital camera directly

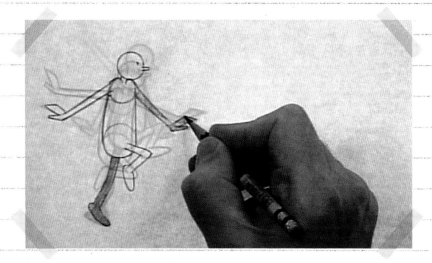

into the computer or else by having each drawing individually scanned and these scanned files then being imported into a movie editing program (such as Premiere or Final Cut Pro) for final rendering.

3D Animation

The process of computer-aided 3D animation is not entirely dissimilar to that of traditional 2D animation. However, remember that we are not talking about the tools of production here. Rather, we are more focused on an approach to creating acceptable and believable action. Therefore, many of these core principles of movement are identical; only the tools are different. Remember too that many of today's finest Pixar animators evolved directly from Disney's traditional animation system, so in reality there really is little to choose from between these two great disciplines, save for a little technical variation.

1. **Understand what you need to achieve.** This part of the process is identical in all forms of animation. Unless you know and recognize what the needs of your scene are—or indeed the needs of a character's role in that scene—you are very much at risk of falling short of what is required.

2. **Rough thumbs.** Again, as with the 2D process, thoroughly explore the acting and performance possibilities of your scene by way of creating a sequence of rough thumbnail sketches of what you want to attempt. Here again, reference footage from real life (or video reference footage of you performing the actions yourself) will provide you with a great deal of reliable material to build on. I always suggest to my students that what they get out of a project is in direct proportion to what they put into it, especially in terms of up-front preparation. Therefore, the more references you can seek out and call on, the better your animation will ultimately become. Never accept simply your own first-thought ideas, since these can always be improved on.

3. **Final thumbs.** When you are more certain of what you want to achieve, draw up more complete, final thumbnail key poses of the gestured action you plan to create. These will provide a valuable reference for what you have to achieve in the 3D environment.

Note:

You might feel that you don't have sufficient drawing skills to take on this thumbnail approach to animation prep—and that's understandable. However, it is my firm belief that by improving your drawing skills—even if you never intend to be a traditional 2D animator—you will greatly enhance your understanding of the dynamics of form, motion, and gesture, and therefore your ability to communicate what you understand will be greatly improved.

4. **3D blocked-in poses.** Now translate your final thumbnail gestures into more conventional 3D ones. You should do this using held (or stepped) splines. These kinds of blocked-in poses will quickly enable you to get a sense of the core action you will be attempting, especially when you can take advantage of the immediate playback opportunity that 3D software provides. Play back your key poses using approximate timing and no in-betweens at this stage. That way you'll get a genuine sense of what's happening with your character action in real screen time but without the distraction of the in-betweens weakening its effect. Remember too that you should always push the dynamic expression in your poses to the maximum and always pay attention to balance and continuity of the kind of character action you are producing—not just from the one viewpoint but all viewpoints.

5. **Breakdown positions.** When you are happy with the action and flow of your key-pose gestures, add all the required breakdown poses and test again by playing it back sans in-betweens until all is working well. Don't forget things like arcs and the fact that not all elements in a character's action move the same distance or at the same speed.

6. **Show blocking to the director.** If you are working on a major production, this is the point at which you show blocking to the director for approval. If you are working alone, then of course the final decision lies entirely with you.

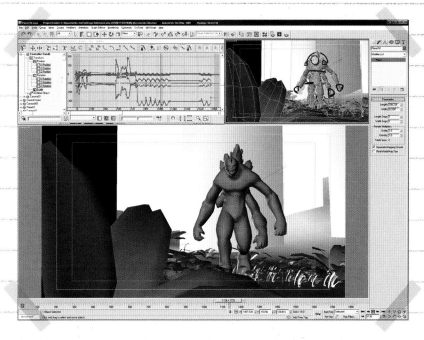

7. **Rework key and breakdown poses.** If you or the director needs to make changes, this is the time to rework your keys and breakdown gestures. Test again and repeat the process until everything is approved. When this happens, it is time to include the in-betweens and see how things look when played back in full motion.

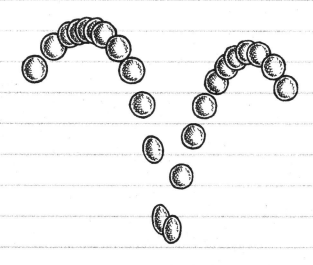

8. **Translate held splines into Bezier splines.** With your in-betweens now included, you are able to polish your animation in a graph editor by adjusting your timing, motion paths, and other subtle elements of movement (to be discussed in other notebook

tutorials). Always remember that although the temptation is instinctively to let the computer dictate most of the in-betweening action for you, it is only by getting in among each individual in-between frame that you can fully realize the potential of your character action. (Important: In-betweening is not a passive process to which an animator should surrender. Not all aspects of a character's movement should be contained by the same keys or with the same placements or tempo. Consequently, you will almost certainly have to make many minute adjusts to your in-betweens as you go along, before your action can be realized to its full potential. This is what separates the animated men from the boys!

9. **Final animation.** Render your final animation for director approval (if required), and then move on to the next scene and begin the whole process again.

Principles of Animation

Animation is universally created using a system of keys, breakdowns (or passing positions, in the case of walks), and in-betweens. Occasionally an animator will work straight ahead, which is a process requiring the animator to create the first position of a sequence and then make successive positional changes to this sequence until the entire action is complete. This is usually the domain of claymation or stop-frame animators. However, the vast majority of 2D and 3D animators around the world uses the keys, breakdowns, and in-betweens approach, since this approach is far more controllable than any other, especially on demanding, larger-scale productions.

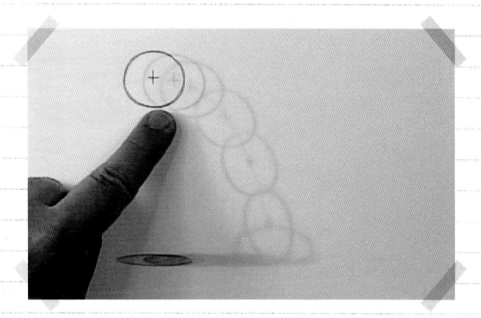

Key positions are the major turning or identifying points in any action. This means that if a character is making a movement, every significant change of direction or emphasis in that movement is defined by a key position. The linking frames, known as in-betweens, or tweens, are not as important as key positions because they are merely transition positions that link one key to another. Consequently, key animators in the traditional 2D genre are principally responsible for defining all the key drawings. The assistant animator, or in-betweener, is responsible for creating all the other drawings. In the 3D world, however, an animator is responsible for creating both key poses and in-betweens.

To better describe the animation process let's use a character turning his head as a suitable example. Check out the film clip on the companion website to see what this action looks like when complete.

As you can see, this action has the head moving from one direction to another. Therefore, the two major key positions in this action will be the first position and the last. Note that this is not the entire movement, just the two positions that define the extreme positions of the movement.

21

The first stage of completing the action after these keys are created is the defining of the **breakdown position**. The breakdown position in this case is the midway location between the two keys. Here is an example of a correct breakdown position in our example.

Note that in this particular version the breakdown position is not precisely in the middle of the two key positions; it is positioned at the bottom of an arc between the two. If it were a literal in-between, it would look like this.

The breakdown drawing in our example is positioned at the bottom of an arc because this gives a more natural action compared with the more robotic feel there would be if we used a literal in-between. Always remember that everything in life moves in arcs—that is, unless it is a very fixed, inflexible action such as that in a machine. Consequently, when you add an arc to a breakdown position, you must always make sure that the **in-betweens** that accompany it follow that arc, too. Here's what the arced path of action looks like in this particular case.

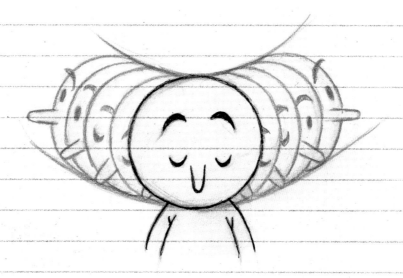

The other thing to remember is that no action (outside the purely mechanical) travels at an even momentum; it is either accelerating or decelerating, or a combination of both. However, for this first example we will use seven evenly placed in-betweens to link the two key positions.

Evenly spaced in-betweens indicate that the action is moving evenly as a result. Therefore, if we want to show this visually, we can draw up an animator's in-betweening chart, like this.

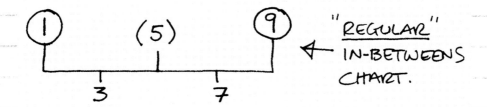

Animation charts such as this one are written onto the key drawings by key animators to indicate to their assistant or in-betweener how they want the linking between drawings to be positioned. Because all the in-betweens are equally spaced in this case, this chart would be known as an equal **in-between chart**.

There are other kinds of timing charts used by key animators, but we will deal with these in Chapter 2, "The Generic Walk," as well as elsewhere in this book. Therefore, for the sake of clarity in this introductory section, we will just consider using equal in-betweens throughout.

Keys

As we said before, the pose is everything in animation! This is the one thing that any animator worth his or her salt has to remember. No matter how cleverly a character is designed, no matter how beautifully it is drawn or how perfect the in-betweens are, if the key poses are not well observed, are out of balance, or are not dynamic enough, the animation will always be under par.

Therefore, when you create your key poses, always think of the dynamics, balance, and message that every key needs to communicate to the audience at every point of the action. Each one of your key poses has to tell a story, needs to be in balance, or needs to have the necessary drive in its structure to imply the precise emotion or personality you are attempting to communicate. Bad poses lead to bad animation, and vice versa. Therefore, give each pose you create the attention and respect it deserves.

Storytelling Keys

We should add here that a number of prominent animators work first with what they call storytelling keys. Storytelling keys are the major gesture positions in which a character will be placed to essentially tell the core story within a scene. Other keyframe positions may be required to support the main action, but the core storytelling keys are the ones that describe it initially.

Other key (or 'extreme') positions might next be added to these, such as an anticipation before the reach down, an extended pose beyond the last position, and so on—but the key storytelling keys remain the first ones to be created.

Note too that in traditional 2D animation, all the numbers of each key drawing are circled to identify them as a key position, but the storytelling keys are often double-circled to indicate that they have the greater emphasis.

Breakdowns

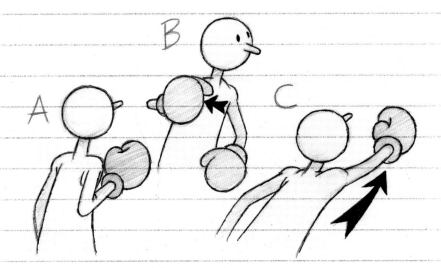

With the key poses in place, it is now time to add the first in-between position between them. This is known as the breakdown position. As we established previously, even though the breakdown position is effectively the midway point between each key, it is rarely in fact precisely that. Returning to our turning head example, let's remind ourselves where the midway breakdown position is.

Sometimes animators need to give the effect of an action having more impact at the front or the end of its movement. To do this they will have to change the position of the breakdown position in the middle. Moving it before the midway position will give the action more speed at the end of the movement, and moving it after the original midway position will add more speed at the beginning. This is how the breakdown position will look if more speed is required at the end of the head turn.

This is where the breakdown drawing will be located if more speed is to be emphasized at the beginning.

Of course, a great deal will depend on where all the other in-betweens are spaced and how many of them there are. However, the above will apply if the in-betweens required are charted as even.

Charts

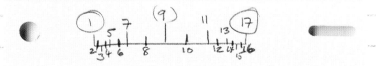

Before we go any further, let's talk a little about charts. In traditional 2D animation, charts are added to a key drawing to define the number of in-betweens the key animator requires for the next key position. Animators who work in 3D can draw up charts, too, to help them work out how they want the movement between two key frames to appear. Let's remind ourselves what an even in-between chart for our head turn looks like.

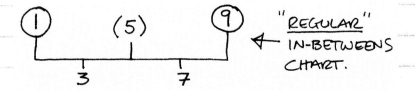

However, most movements are neither constant nor even. As indicated earlier, pretty much all motion is in a process of either accelerating or decelerating, or both. The secret for the animator is to identify what is required for the actions he or she is working on and to adapt in-betweens accordingly. The notion of slowing in and slowing out is discussed elsewhere in this book, but for now let us state that if an action is accelerating, a slowing out of the in-between will be necessary. Here's the head turn chart for a slowing-out action.

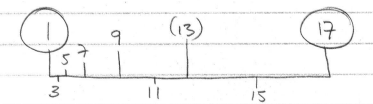

And here's the same chart where a slowing-in (decelerating) in-betweening action is indicated.

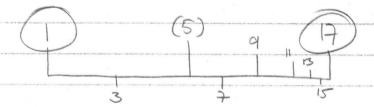

Note that the big difference between them is the way that the in-betweens are distributed. The more in-betweens there are, the slower an action will go. Therefore, when there are more in-betweens indicated at the beginning of the action (slowing out), the slower the start of the action is, and vice versa.

The Importance of Testing

Remember, it is extremely important for animators to test and review their work regularly as they go along. In all honesty it is very, very rare for any animator to get things right on the first attempt. Consequently, the process of animation is very much one of trial and error. So testing everything as you go along is strongly advised. For traditional 2D animators, regular "flipping" of their drawings is a must.

Flipping

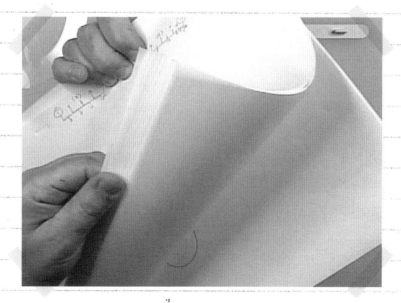

Flipping is where an animator holds up a stack of animation drawings (lowest numbers at the bottom, highest at the top) and views them as they flip rapidly from bottom to top. Flipping gives a sense of how an entire action is shaping up before it is formally shot. It doesn't necessarily give a perfect representation of how the action will appear in real time on a screen, but it does give a strong overall impression of how it will look. Here's another example of scene flipping.

Sometimes traditional animators will want to check just the few drawings they are working on rather than an entire sequence. In this case, peg flipping, or rolling, as it is sometimes called, is used. Traditional animators need to use registration pegs to synchronize their drawings one to another. They will either position these pegs at the top of the drawing (top pegs animation) or at the bottom (bottom pegs animation), depending on preference. Peg flipping therefore is a process of interweaving the fingers between the drawings and flipping them in sequence to see how it is moving. Here's an example of peg flipping for bottom peg animators.

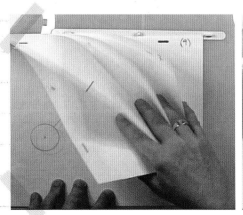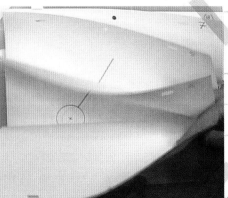

And here is an example of top peg flipping.

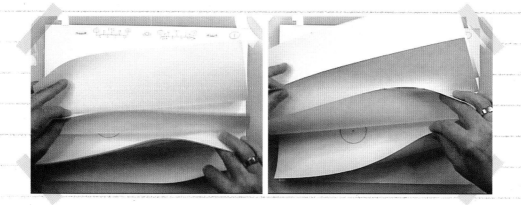

Playback Testing

All types of animators will need to test their work by playback before anyone signs off on it. Most traditional animation software, as well as 3D animation software, allows animators to play back their animation in real time, whether that real time is at 24 fps (frames per second), 25fps, or 30 fps. However, whatever system of animation is being attempted, the regular playing back of animation is of paramount importance, and clearly, the more the animators test and refine their work, the better it ultimately will be.

Timing and Spacing

We should now briefly talk about timing and spacing. These things come best with experience, but there are basic guidelines that will help even the most novice animator.

More Means Slower!

Animators ultimately have the power to do everything they want when it comes to timing. However, there are a few factors that should always be borne in mind. The first is the reminder that the more drawings or positions there are between keys, the slower

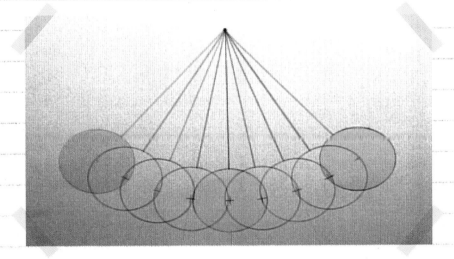

the action will be. Alternatively, the fewer drawings or positions there are, the faster that action will be. Here's the chart of our head turn example, first with the original number of in-between drawings added (blue) and then with twice as many in-betweens added (red).

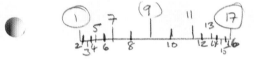

Traditional animators have the added potential of putting in one drawing per frame (animation on one's) or sometimes one drawing for every two frames (animation on two's). Usually animation on one's is reserved for theatrical movies and animation on two's is reserved for TV and video productions. Web animation usually has more frames per drawing. The ideal-world situation is that if an action is animated on one's it will tend to be smoother and richer to look at.

What Not to Do

When animating for the first time, never take shortcuts. Obey the rules. Do things the hard way. It is only by learning the rules and applying them that you'll know how to break them later, when you are more experienced. Breaking rules in ignorance means that you

may actually get away with things for 1 percent of the time. But for the other 99 percent of the time, your animation will inevitably look poor and underwhelming. Therefore, don't take shortcuts—such as using two's when you should be using one's or putting in fewer in-betweens when you should really be adding more. Remember, what you get out of a project is in direct proportion to what you put in. The screen is a harsh judge of your work, and if the material is simply not there in the first place, it will not suddenly appear when you play it back!

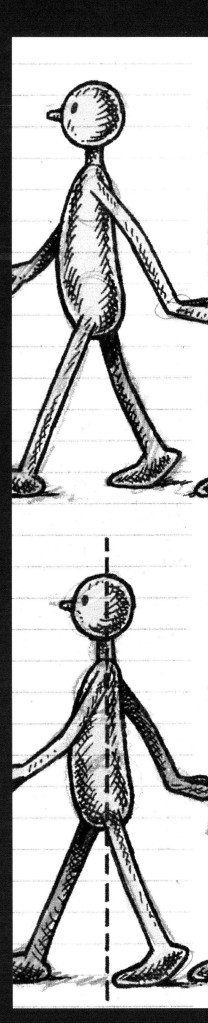

chapter 2

The Generic Walk

A standard dictionary interpretation of the word walk might go something like this: "The manner in which a two-legged creature moves by placing one foot in front of the other to gain momentum, usually forward momentum."

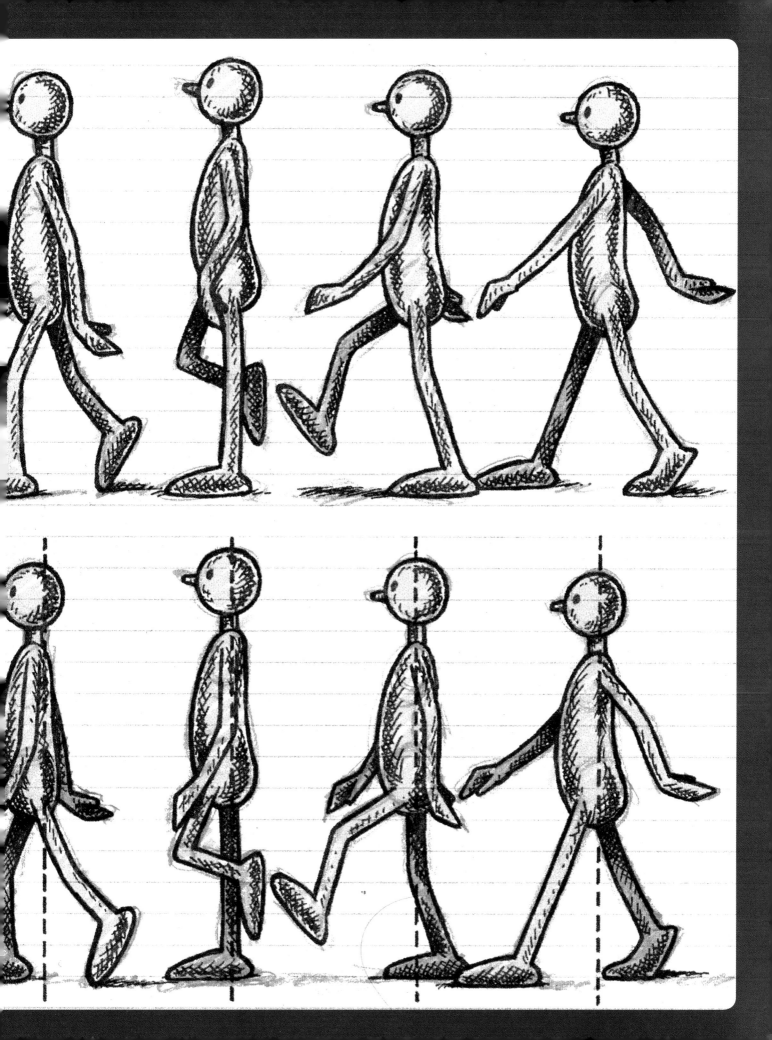

A more clearly defined explanation for animators is that a walk is an action, usually with a moving biped character (but not necessarily so), where one foot is always in contact with the ground at any moment in time.

The one-foot-on-the-ground rule is actually in keeping with the USATF rule for competitive race walking, which states that "race walking is a progression of steps so taken that the walker makes contact with the ground so that no visible [to the human eye] loss of contact occurs. The advancing leg must be straightened [i.e., not bent at the knee] from the moment of first contact with the ground until in the vertical upright position." Animators should not necessarily take the "straight advancing leg" definition to heart, but the bottom line is that there is always one foot in contact with the ground at any particular moment in time within the movement.

Note how a race walker never loses touch with the ground at any particular moment in time!

If for any reason both feet consistently leave the ground at the same time, that action is more accurately defined as a run or a jump, depending on the nature of the action.

Walks apply to quadruped characters too, but that will be the subject of a separate chapter later. For the rest of these particular notes, we will continue to refer to biped action only.

The Challenge

All the great animators with whom I have studied in the past have always told me that a good walk is the hardest thing for any animator to pull off. It is said that all the principles inherent in a walk, when fully understood, will be found in all other aspects of animated action—arcs, weight, timing, overlapping action, and so on. Consequently, if an animator learns to pull off a good animated walk convincingly, I would say that animator should be able to pull off anything in animation, making what follows even more important to understand!

We will study the process of creating an animated walk shortly, but first let's look back in time for a moment.

Drawing from History

It goes without saying that the action of walking has challenged animators since the very beginnings of our industry. Initially, in the Fleischer era, animators' characters walked with no consistent form, weight, or balance in their action.

I illustrated this in my film *Endangered Species* by reproducing the "Bimbo" walk with my own Animaticus-styled character.

In early animation, "rubber hose" animation meant that cartoon characters apparently had no skeletal structure inside their bodies and therefore their arms and legs flopped around like rubber hoses.

Of course, as time evolved and audiences became more familiar with the novelty aspects of animated cartoon characters, the rubber-hose technique went out of style and animators began to consider more characters that had some kind of consistent anatomy, form, and rigidity of bones and joints. This in itself led to a different form of animation, where the notion of plausible implausibility was embraced. Walt Disney was at the forefront of this movement. Indeed, as with pretty much everything else that related to animated movement and filmmaking, this new evolution of the nature of animated walks evolved from the work of animators at the emerging Disney studio, a tradition that was consolidated and extended through the work of what is now defined as the Golden Age. When Walt was alive and spearheading the studio, he encouraged artists and animators to consider the science of movement as well as cartoon action as a novelty and essentially an imaginative art form.

As a result of this more mature and naturalistic refocusing, animated characters began more and more to appear as though they were real. They became much more well-rounded in a three-dimensional sense (although we are still talking about traditional 2D animation, of course), and their bodily dimensions and movements were much more defined by a more natural, imagined skeleton within the body. The joint movements were more consistent with human action, too, since Walt began to see his animated worlds as still fantasy driven but nevertheless reflecting what we're used to in real life. This is when the core formulas for the generic walk action were defined and even where the nature and structure of his greatest character ever, Mickey Mouse, significantly evolved.

The Basic Principles

With this chapter we are essentially dealing with the generic walk only. A generic walk can be broken down into a very few essential principles that, once understood, can be the foundations of all animated walks, whether generic or otherwise.

With any kind of biped walk there are two principal key stride positions—that is, left leg forward and right leg forward. These appear as follows.

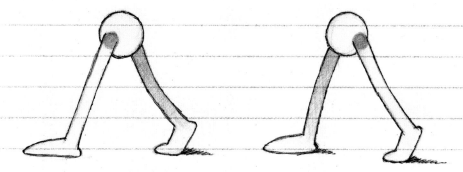

With the legs established, the next principle to understand is that when the right leg is forward the left arm is forward, and when the left leg is forward the right arm is forward. The arms and legs are therefore counterposal.

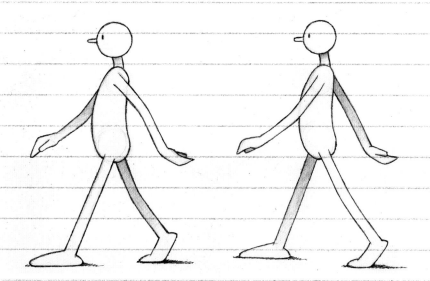

Between the two key-pose stride positions is a midstride position, known as the **passing position**. The passing position is that point where the rear leg of the first key-pose position is midway to moving forward to being the front leg in the next key-pose position.

Remember that the contact foot (that is, the foot that is on the ground during a stride action) will always remain on the floor leading up to, during, and after the passing

position, until the next key-pose stride position is established. The leg coming through from front to back, and which is not on the ground, is known as the free leg. I tend to call the passing position in a generic walk action the "number 4" position, since its shape approximately describes the number 4.

Also, one of the most important things about the passing position (and this is often neglected in very bad walk actions) is that the entire torso rises upward in relation to the key stride positions. This is pure geometry because, when the angled leg on a stride position angles to a vertical position, the body is forced to rise.

Another really important factor that is ignored in less successful walking actions is the fact that before the rear leg finally leaves the ground to move toward the passing position, it is preferable to keep the toe on the ground for as long as possible. This gives a greater sense of dynamic push to the action of the rear leg, which, after all, is responsible for much of the forward motion and direction of the walk.

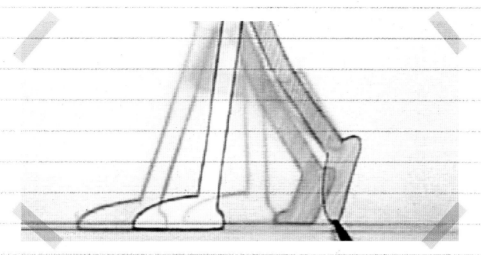

Also, before the free foot makes contact with the ground on the next key stride position, it will swing a little higher and a little more forward than the eventual point of contact. If you walk yourself and examine what happens when you bring your own foot forward and down, you see that it tends to swing forward and up before your heel eventually hits the ground at the end of the stride.

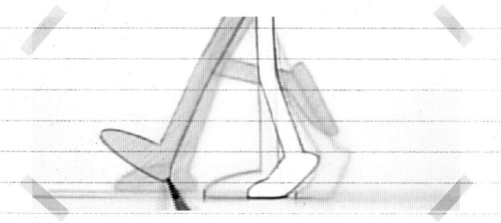

As indicated, the foot usually tends to contact the ground with the heel first, before the rest of the foot follows through by dropping down into its normal flat position. Sometimes this will not happen if a more stub toe effect is needed (such as a baby learning to walk for the first time), but in 99 percent of generic walks the heel-to-toe action on the contact foot is more natural.

Remember, too, that for all generic walk positions, to maintain a balanced sense of momentum in the action at all times it is important that the center of gravity within the character's body mass always be positioned above the contact foot position when the free leg is off the ground; otherwise it should be positioned between both points of contact when both feet are on the ground at the same time (such as with the key stride positions).

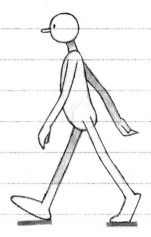

Unless a drunkard's walk is being attempted, good balance over the contact foot is always essential when an animator is seeking to create a natural, balanced walk. This key principle applies to walks seen from the front as well as the back views. Without this important balance being emphasized, the positions of the walk will look unnatural and out of balance, and therefore the audience will not feel it convincing (even if that feeling is on a subconscious level and not a conscious one).

The Arms

Moving away from the legs and body, we must now consider the arms. As an arm moves forward on its swing, it will have a greater sense of naturalness and flexibility if the hand drags a little behind the forearm. So, as the arm moves forward, the hand should be held back a little, as though dragging behind, only flipping over at the very end when the arm changes direction.

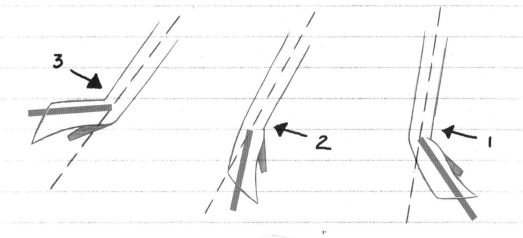

Similarly, when the arm moves backward on its swing, the hand can be held back to appear as though it is dragging a little behind the forearm until it flips over as the arm changes direction again. This will again emphasize a sense of flexibility to the entire action.

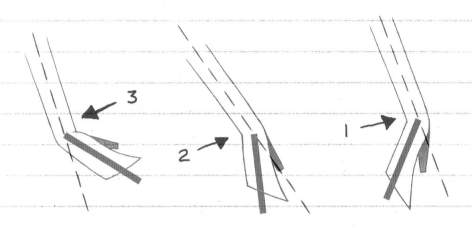

Note

There will be a point of transition at which the hand dragging back in one swing direction suddenly begins to drag back in the opposite direction as the arm swing reverses. In such cases, do not in-between the hand so that it is in a straight line with the forearm. Instead, favor one side of the center line position or the other, as this will give the whole action a little more natural ''snap.'' This principle applies to all in-betweens that go from a basic convex shape to a concave shape (i.e., straight lines indicate weakness in animation terms, and straight in-betweens therefore will suggest the same thing).

Body Action

Now we have to deal with the natural fluidity and flexibility within the body. Note that when an arm moves forward on a swing, the shoulder will tend to rotate forward too. Then when the arm moves backward, the shoulder also rotates backward in relation to the body. To not do this will give a rigidness to the action and will suggest that the shoulder is more of a fixed hinge rather than a fluid, natural joint.

This also applies to the lower torso. When a leg reaches forward on the stride, the hip also moves forward. Similarly, when the leg moves back in contact with the ground, the hip moves back with it. This inherent limb-related movement in the hips and the shoulders gives a natural sense of twist in the torso that will make the character less stiff and less cut-out looking.

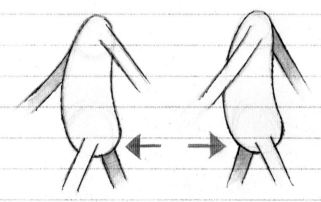

The Head

Finally, to bring additional flexibility to the generic walk, we need to consider the head action. Right now it is just moving up and down with the body, but with the more fluid and flexible neck connecting the two, it needs some special additional attention too. So, when the body rises up on the passing position, it will help the overall action considerably to have the head tilt downward a little on the rise. This will suggest some flexibility in the neck joint.

Similarly, when the body starts to move down between the passing position and the next stride position, it will loosen things up even more if the head tilts upward a little more as the body sinks. The combined overlapping action on the head as the body rises and falls will ensure that the character moves in a more natural and effective way.

Body Lean

Of course, each one of these principles will amount to nothing if the figure doing the walking does not have a means of motivation. By motivation we mean the element that naturally drives a moving figure. Most people assume that it is the back leg driving off that gives momentum. To some extent it does, but without added body lean, the character will not be able to continue beyond the first step after the push-off. Body lean is what enables us to move. Too much body lean causes us to fall flat on our faces!

Do this experiment yourself. Stand still and upright and lift one foot up, balancing on the other. What happens? Correct: Nothing (other than your foot lifting up, that is!). Now do the same thing as you lift your foot up, but this time lean forward as you do it—that is, go one step beyond your balance comfort zone. What happens this time? Correct: You step forward one stride. Now, if you keep leaning forward and lift the other foot as the first one contacts the ground—you are starting to walk! That's exactly what you did when you were a baby, although you were no doubt so uncoordinated in those days that at first you didn't get your free leg down and balanced and you inevitably fell flat on your face!

Consequently, when you animate your walk, make sure that there is a degree of body lean on the body as your character moves. If the body is perfectly upright, your audience will not buy your walk for one minute. Give it a slight lean and they will. The degree to which your character leans is dependent on the speed at which you want your character to walk. The greater the lean, the faster the character will walk. The less the lean, the less the speed of the walk and the less distance in stride length your character will have to stretch to make it convincing.

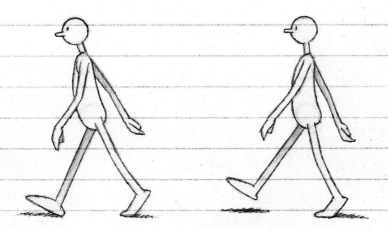

The Final Walk

Now, to see all these principles working together and in action, view the video to see what a competent generic walk looks like when seen as a standard walk cycle. Remember, though, in this lesson we will not be looking for personality or emotion in the walk—just the generic foundational movement that a basic walk like this is required to have. This action was shot on two's (each drawing shot for two frames of film) and looks like this.

Variations

Even with a generic walk there can be variations that will give your walk a little something different. For example, you can delay the passing leg a little to get a very different look to the entire action. This will provide for a slightly slower pickup from the back position and a faster, more dynamic hit to the foot on the plant-down at the front.

On the other hand, here's what it looks like when you advance the leg in the passing position to create a faster back pickup and a slower, slightly more studied planting action.

You can get more bounciness to the walk if you push the body up higher (i.e., up onto the toes of the contact foot) in the passing position. The extra height means that the up-and-down variations on the head and body are exaggerated, therefore giving it a greater bouncing effect.

Alternatively, if you want to give a flatter, less exaggerated bounce to the walk, you can lessen the height of the body on the passing position. (Although if you remove the up-and-down action entirely, you will lose the effect of a generic walk, making it look more like a generic glide!)

Again, let's remind ourselves of what might happen if the poses of the action are out of balance. Here's an extreme example of what happens if the body mass is not over the points of contact throughout the movement. It is amusing in a cartoon sort of way, but hardly convincing in a realistic way!

Timing

Up to this point we've indicated what might be termed **even** timing action. Even timing actions imply that the in-between positions are equal from key stride to key stride and there is no variation of location or number of drawings used. If we indicate what this means through a standard traditional animator's key chart, this is how even timing would look in terms of the in-betweens required. This will give an action that moves evenly too, with no timing variations or emphasis.

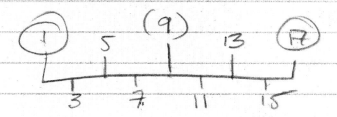

However, if we add more in-betweens at the end or at the beginning of an action (known as slowing in and slowing out), we get a very different feel to the walk. Here is a key chart that integrates both a slow-out and a slow-in.

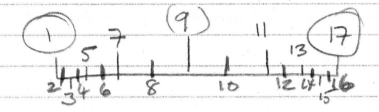

To illustrate this idea, here's a chart that has more slow-in and slow-out drawings created around the passing position.

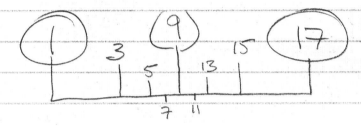

Now check the animation on www.animatorsnotebook.com to see what it looks like in movement.

On the other hand, here's a chart that shows more slow-in and slow-out in-betweens created around the key stride positions.

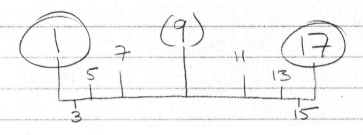

Now check the companion website to see how it differs from the previous example.

Remember what these drawing placement differences look like in real-time movement and consider using these kinds of timing techniques when you are producing your own animated action, whether a walk animation or not.

Front Walks

Now we are in a computer graphics (CG) world where all animation, including walks, can potentially be viewed through 360 degrees, with anything from a high to low viewpoint. So it is necessary for us to consider a generic walk from the front as well as the side plane. If we can at least get these walks right, all the other optional angles will be easier to deal with from a more 3D point of view.

In terms of action, the movement of a generic walk from the front is identical to a generic walk action from the side. The only thing a 2D animator has to consider, however, is the perspective of the limbs as they come to and go from the viewer. In other words, when a foot or a hand comes forward, it will grow appreciably larger in the screen, whereas when it goes away from the viewer, it will appear to become smaller.

That aside, the crucial thing that all animators must take into account when viewing a walk from any angle other than a pure profile shot is that the balance of the character's center of gravity will move from side to side on the step. The notion of the body weight always being over the point of contact with the ground is increasingly important too. Most inexperienced animators of all kinds tend to ignore this idea. They may successfully put in an up-and-down movement from the stride to the passing positions, but their walk will lose a great deal of its naturalness if there is no side shifting either. For example, there is a generic walk seen from the front that simply goes up and down on its central plane on the companion website.

It works okay, but it's hardly natural. The key thing that must never be forgotten in a walk or with any other action that requires one foot to leave the ground is that **the body mass must first adjust itself over the main contact foot before the free leg can become free**. To not do that will communicate to the audience that the character is not in balance or is not subject to the normal rules of gravity. Consequently, as a character takes a new stride, its body weight must be transferred over the contact leg before the free leg can be lifted from the ground and moved forward. On the companion website, you can find an exaggerated example of this concept, to get the point across.

Note how the body weight shift actually holds back as the free leg is lifted up and into the passing position, and it is **only when that leg is planted forward** that the body mass tends to shift forward and across with it until it firmly takes the body weight in its own right. Everything else about this action is identical to our standard generic walk, except that with the weight shift it now appears far more natural and convincing!

What Not to Do

When you're starting to animate for the first time, it is okay for you to make many mistakes. That is the only way you'll learn and the only way you'll get experience of what animation is about. So don't stress if what you try does not come off exactly as you imagine it in your mind at first. It ultimately will, especially when you get numerous attempts at walk action under your belt.

But be warned: There are many common faults that make walks look unconvincing or simply bad to the beginner! At www.animatorsnotebook.com, you'll find some common errors that you will probably make when producing your first walks—although by highlighting them here, perhaps we can help you avoid making these kinds of errors!

The first example is what it looks like when there are **no opposing arms and legs** in a walk (i.e., the right arm is forward when the right leg is forward).

The next walk is what it looks like if you absolutely **don't have any "up" movement** on the passing position.

The final walk example is what it looks like if you **don't keep the toe down on the back leg** after the key stride position, or **reach up and forward** before the front contact position.

Suggested Assignment

Now it's time for you to prove that you understand the principles of creating a generic walk by animating one yourself! Feel free to either use the simply yellow character featured in this book or create a character design of your own. When you've finished your animation, film it and seek out an experienced animator to give you feedback on your work. There are many Internet forums online that you can use to make this contact. Or else you may be lucky enough to have a professional animator locally who can advise you.

chapter 3

Stylized Walks

In the previous chapter about generic walks we discussed how animators are able to create a standard, failsafe walk that will work for any biped character that needs to be animated. Now we must begin to dig deeper into our animator's chest of goodies to find ways of expressing personality and emotion through the walks our characters do. Think about it: We all walk in the same way—one leg in front of the other, arms opposing the leg action—but it is the body language of our walk that defines our personality, our mood, and even our intention. Even a scant look at the people walking in a local shopping mall or main street will confirm just how differently people express themselves through the manner in which they walk. Note how people who are confident, nervous, sad, happy, arrogant, or humble visibly define themselves as they make their way from place to place. All these things need to be observed and then expressed in the "personality" walks we animate.

The Pose (or Gesture) Is Everything

It is pretty much universally accepted by the finest animators that what separates great animation from so-so animation are those little touches that add up to bringing true character and feeling to the action. This effectively means getting strong and evocative poses when keying the action out. Even in basic walks it is perfectly possible to communicate mood, emotion, and personality through the kinds of key frame gestures (or poses) you establish. This notion is referred to in other chapters too.

For example, here are three stride poses that communicate different aspects of a character's mood or personality.

Note that we haven't even moved anything, yet already the character begins to speak to us, simply through the pose. This is why the pose is everything in animation!

Other Conditioning Factors

There are other factors that will influence the way a character walks.

Weight

Simply by the character's weight alone there will be an adjustment in the action. For example, a heavy character (or a character carrying a heavy weight) will tend to have a little give in his front leg action after the foot presses down. For example, when the lead

foot hits the ground (usually heel first), the weight, mass, and velocity of the character's body (or whatever he is carrying) will tend to force a slight bend in the lead knee—very much like the nature of a shock absorber in a car when that car hits a bump. The leg will straighten up again pretty much by the time it reaches the passing position, but that little touch will give added authenticity and weight to the character in question. Here is an example of how the three key positions might look, from the hit to the passing position.

Weight Dispersal

Other natural factors taking place in an animated walk might influence just how that character will move. For example, with a human walk there are three aspects to the contact foot when it hits the ground. The first is that the heel will usually come down first, followed by the weight being dispersed along the outside of the foot, and then finally the weight is transferred to the front, across the toe area. Here's an example of what occurs in diagrammatic form.

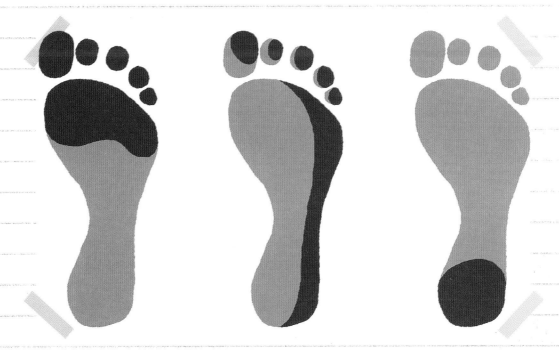

This could possibly affect the way you pose your character around that kind of walk action. To overemphasize it could suggest a character that is walking slowly and in a bow legged way, for example, or clumsily and lead-footed if you ignore it by maybe going the other way.

Balance

Remember too that whatever you do with a personality walk, the character's body weight needs to be over the point (or points) of contact at all times (unless that character is uncoordinated, drunk, or about to fall over for some reason). This rule not only applies to the profile axis of the action but also includes a front axis view or indeed the full 360-degree view of a character walking. For example:

Any one of these basic factors will immediately begin to lift your generic walk to a more advanced level—and we haven't even addressed mood, emotion, or personality yet!

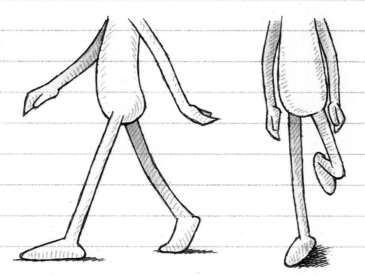

As I repeatedly say, a successful walk is a hard thing for an animator to master, and a personality walk is even harder. That said, there are little tricks of the trade that will help animators take their walks beyond the generic. Let's start with the cliché—techniques and styles that will give you some formulas to work with. These can be used as they are, or aspects of them can be used to give a certain emotional or personality effect.

Double-Bounce Walk

Now let's get down to the nitty-gritty of stylized walks. The early and immediately recognizable Mickey Mouse walk was known as the double-bounce walk. The double-bounce walk produced the happy, bouncy, and confident Mickey that everyone knew and loved at that time. At the heart of it, the double-bounce walk is simply a manipulation of the generic walk's core principles. On the website, you'll see an example of what a standard double-bounce walk looks like from the hips downward.

On the surface there are a lot of complicated elements going on here, but at the heart of it there is one simple formula that needs to be observed: The character actually moves **down on the passing position and up on the in-betweens**!

Note, however, that although the body position is kept artificially down on the passing position and up on the in-between positions, the legs are not distorted in either size or volume in any way. The up-and-down effect is easily achieved by the knees being bent

down farther than normal on the passing position and the character is pushed up on its toes for the in-between stretches.

Of course, to get variation and personality in the walk, away from the double-bounce effect, these kinds of simple rules can be bent in other ways. For example, try keeping the body down on the first in-between position and up on the second in-between position.

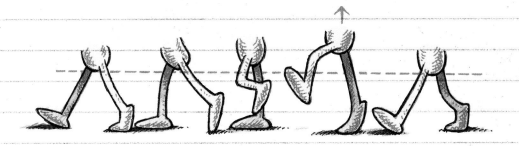

Or up on the first in-between position and down on the second.

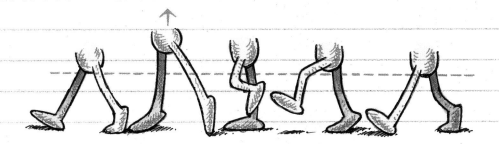

These simple changes will give two entirely different senses of personality to the walking action.

There are other ways of achieving variation in the generic walk to give emotion or personality, such as pose variation, breakdown position manipulation, creative approaches to the overlapping action, weight, arcs, flowing paths of action, and so on. Let's examine a few more now.

Key Positions

Remember that everything is in the pose. So always make sure your key stride positions tell the story you want to communicate. For example, which of the following poses we illustrated earlier do you think suggest "normal," "eccentric," and "sad"?

Clearly, even without any movement in place, the characters are already displaying characteristics of mood and personality without the viewer's even thinking about how they move. Actually, the nature of the pose that is established up front will affect the way the character will move.

Now let's take just one of the actions—sad, for example—and examine how the rest of the in-betweens might be defined. Remember, there are still infinite options for an animator to consider here, even within the broad category of "sad walk." The example you'll find at www.animatorsnotebook.com is just one acceptable suggestion.

The animation example is what it looks like when played back in real time.

In-Betweens

Remember that when you're attempting any animation, it is not merely a question of putting in mechanical in-between positions. Nothing in life, other than a very fixed machine, moves evenly; everything moves on arcs, is accelerating or decelerating, and has eccentric movements that, especially in the case of walks, don't even necessarily coincide with the main key frame timings. As one outstanding Pixar animator once said to my students, "There's no 'magic button' in software that makes things move for you. You have to get in there and work on every single frame in its own way, especially when working with 3D animation software."

Let's take this concept further and look at this sequence of a character walking down steps that I based on an analysis of Mickey Mouse's walk in the wonderful "Sorcerer's Apprentice" sequence in *Fantasia* (see the website for the animated example).

Notice how there is an overall emphasis on the "up" passing position. In other words, as with a traditional bouncing-ball principle, there is a slow-in and slow-out placement of the in-betweens around the upper, passing position of the stride, as we illustrated in the "Generic Walk" notebook tutorial.

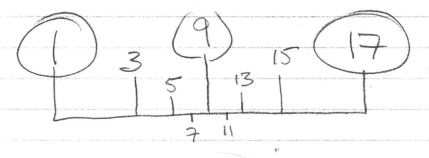

Also note that when the free foot comes through on the passing position, the placement is as normal, but when the foot comes down to the hit position, the toe leads, giving a softer, more precise contact with the ground.

Notice, too, the arms move through on wide, sweeping arcs with, again, a slow-in/slow-out effect at the top of each swing.

The combined effect of all this movement is to create a bouncy, perky walk that gives a sense of fun and yet control to the action as the character descends the stairs. Note the charm I added when he throws a backward glance at the very end, taking the whole thing off from the predictable and repetitive.

Now contrast all this to a typical Max Fleischer-inspired style of walk, epitomized by an early "rubber hose" style of character, somewhat like Bimbo.

In analyzing this action, I noted that although there is some kind of personality to the walk, it is still generic in nature and yet does not conform to the kinds of disciplines we have discussed here and elsewhere in this book.

First, note the lack of balance to the stride and that the character's body weight is not over the point of contact at all times, giving a sense that the character is either leaning or falling backward.

Also note a consistent change of shape and length of legs that was a mark of the rubber hose era. I hat said, there was wonderful animation created in that time, albeit a very different sort from the structural and anatomical disciplines we are subject to today.

Sneaks

Perhaps there is no more common example of a widely recognizable stylized walk than the sneak. There are three kinds of sneaks: the slow sneak, the fast sneak, and the backward sneak (as defined in my *Animation from Pencils to Pixels: Classical Techniques for Digital Animators*). We will deal with the first two here; the latter type is effectively a reversal of the first.

Slow Sneak

The action of the slow sneak is pretty standard. The characteristic movements are that the character's body leans far back when the lead leg reaches forward to hit the ground, and then the body bends far forward just before entering the passing position. The rest is a matter of timing.

There are different ways of approaching the arms, but as you have seen in the previous example I've "twinned" them (i.e., made them look and move similarly and together) for the sake of simplicity.

Once you have these key positions worked out, it is simply a matter of in-between placement and timing. With a slow sneak, there will be a lot of in-betweens. On the website, you'll find an example of what it looks like as a final line test.

Also, because this is a stylized action and relies on timing variances to emphasize the main pose positions of the character, the use of slow-ins and slow-outs at the beginning and end of the movement helps significantly. I suggest working with the following charting as a starting point.

Putting this all together, the example on the website shows what the final sneak looks like.

Fast Sneak

The fast sneak is effectively a very quick "tippy-toe" action, where the character barely touches the ground and tries to catch up with and/or get away from another character as quickly and as silently as possible.

The secret to the fast sneak is that it is technically not a walk at all but is actually a run. See how both feet are off the ground at a certain point in time? This is a characteristic that defines a run as opposed to a walk, which, as you should know now, will always have one foot on the ground at any point in time.

Note, too, how there is a very strong up-and-down action, as opposed to forward action on each stride in this rough pencil test.

Timing

One of the most important things about all walks, especially stylized walks, is the variation in timing. With a generic walk there is very little expression in the poses and certainly very little variant timing in the action. Everything on a generic walk tends to be even and predictable. On the website, you'll see a basic walk that I analyzed and recreated from a scene in the *Fritz the Cat* movie. Apart from the unique pen-and-ink design style, see how plain, even, and quite unimaginative the walk action really is.

Also on the website is a similar generic walk I analyzed and recreated from a scene in *Yellow Submarine*. Again, the design style rescues the action, which in itself is very underwhelming and predictable. Not good! Note that there are four very different characters here, but effectively they all walk the same, timing out on the same key frames, each expressing the same action that shows no difference between them except for their color and clothing design.

Now, by contrast, look at the action of a limping character (on the website) and note how varied the weight, timing, and poses are.

The first thing to note on this action is the great difference in timing between the strong stride and the weak one. Here's the difference in number of drawings for a start.

Second, because the character effectively collapses on the weak leg stride and attempts to transfer its weight onto the strong leg as quickly as possible, there is a very big difference in the shape and gesture of the poses involved.

Finally, because this action is similar to a sneak in some ways (for example, with the character ensuring a careful placement of his feet, the use of slow-ins and slow-outs helps communicate the action more clearly to the audience), you will see a similarity in the nature of the timing and charting—at least on the strong leg action. Here's what the charts look like covering both two-stride actions.

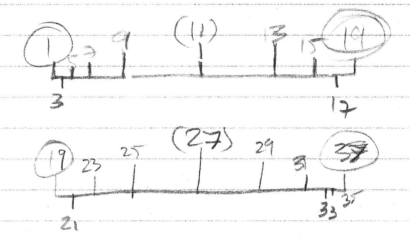

Observe! Observe!! Observe!!!

I can never stress enough that although the preceding guidelines offer simple tips and formulas for creating specific kinds of stylistic walks, it is only through an intense and focused observation of real-life activity that a real and convincing caricature of real-life movement can be achieved through animation. Remember, however, that animation is not a perfect replication of life but rather is a **caricature** of that action. There will always be huge advantages for the animator if he or she invests in significant and tailored observation for reference points before embarking on a scene. With some fantasy action it is impossible to recreate this in real life in many instances, but for so many other things it is possible to either sketch, film, or at least photograph the real-life actions of people doing the very action you are attempting to interpret. There is no substitute for seeking reference, whether it is an animator producing a moving scene or a graphic designer creating a product package.

Real-life research is better than looking up books in a library, but looking up books in a library can often be more effective than simply Googling YouTube or something similar on the Web. Filming your own moves specifically tailored for the action you intend to interpret is easily best, although if you are forced to resort to finding something near to what you want on YouTube, then all well and good!

Most people have access to digital video cameras these days, or at least a still camera that can capture key positions as people move. So why not use these tools to your benefit as an animator? Animators must use all kinds of technology if they can, although to be a slave of technology is not the ideal either. The best approach of all: Sketch your key poses from life, whether you are a 2D or a 3D animator! Through drawing you can more accurately and surely imbue the caricature aspect of the action prior to committing to the key storytelling poses of your proposed animation.

Mo-Cap

Motion capture, or mo-cap, is one example of new technology that is an animator's greatest friend *and* worst enemy! It's our greatest friend because it enables us to capture and analyze, in frame-by-frame, high-speed detail, the precise movement of a figure in action. At the same time, it's our worst enemy because it gives a film or game producer so much opportunity to take the cheap route by converting data to move a premodeled character, thus eliminating the animator entirely. The really strange thing is, though, that mo-cap action, unmodified and untouched by an experienced animator's eye, will always look fake, weak, and wooden. Traditional 2D animators who have seen the same thing attempted by rotoscoping (tracing) live action footage will confirm. That said, check out the example on the website of the kind of action reference that mo-cap footage can provide interested animators, but only as a reference for creating their own superior and enhanced animation.

In-Betweening 2D Animation on One's

Finally, let the 2D animators among us talk for a minute about the value of one's to our animation. These days a great deal of 2D animation is created on two's—maybe more than that with some limited animation examples.

Two's are where each drawing is shot for two frames each. However, when it comes to the best of stylized walks, as with any other action that is subtle or fast moving, it is far more desirable to go for animation on one's (i.e., one drawing for each frame of film).

One's are essential where broad, fast action is involved or where smoothness of movement is extremely important.

Using one's is almost a necessity for theatrical projection, where a huge cinema screen will demand much more smoothness with animated action, since everything is so greatly enlarged and therefore each move from frame to frame is that much more exaggerated.

The old Disney animators would always insist that if two drawings were so far apart that there was no overlap between them on a frame-by-frame basis, an in-betweened frame would have to be inserted between them to smooth the whole thing out from the cinema audience's perspective.

Suggested Assignment

Create a nongeneric stylized walk based on personal observation. Go out into a public place and watch people walking in their own individual ways. Find someone who has a particularly extreme way of walking. Film it or sketch it out, and then attempt to translate that walk into animation with a character of your own design.

Don't forget to use the thumbnail and other processes described earlier for this assignment!

Test and adjust each of your attempts as necessary until you have something that most closely caricatures the real-life walk you originally observed. Then pat yourself on your back when it does!

chapter 4

Personality Walks

In previous chapters we dealt with generic walks and eccentric walks. Now we will get down to the real nitty-gritty—personality walks.

What exactly do we mean by personality walks? Essentially what we are talking about here are walks that are personalized and unique interpretations of individualistic movement with a walking action, or ones that express mood or personality or sometimes even special adaptation to the environment in which the character is moving. Fundamentally though, they are mainly walks that define emotion, character traits, and indeed as their name implies, personality.

Personality walks are walks that are unique to a character, express mood or personality, or indicate a character's adaptation to the environment.

As indicated earlier about generic walks, although we all walk similarly (i.e., one leg in front of the other, arms swinging in opposition to legs), there are in fact no two identical walks on this planet. Like fingerprints we each exert a slightly different imprint on the way we move as we walk, primarily affected by our mood, our physical assets or limitations, the urgency of our action, and indeed anything else in our world that governs the way and the speed at which we do things. For example, a character with an artificial leg will walk in an entirely different way from a character who is supremely fit. A character who is fit will walk entirely differently if he is happy, sad, at leisure, pressed for time, or even on stilts! In each case we will need to factor in varying aspects of the way we interpret a character's generic style of walking to such a point that his walk is uniquely personal to him and him alone—indeed it is the personality walk that is most intimately associated with a character.

In an exercise in Chapter 3 we studied the walk of a sad person. To some degree this was a personality walk, although because it was really only a generic walk altered by pose alone, it is not 100 percent a personality walk in the truest sense of the word. To create a true walk of this type we have to get even further into the personality of the character to examine any physical limitations or advantages and then define how the character will express these in a physical way.

For example, a sad person with a painful walk will certainly tend to limp or drag her foot through the discomfort of putting her weight on that one weaker leg. Indeed this could be why she is sad in the first place. On the other hand, she may be used to the pain of the walk but be saddened by the fact that she can't pay her rent that month, or she is carrying a huge weight on her shoulders. Each piece in the puzzle needs to be factored in before we can decide exactly what that personality walk is all about.

Certainly doing a personality profile and life back-story on the character in your mind first will help flesh out the approach you might take in the way the character walks. Even obtaining the right pose that tells a big story—like the gesture style we employed in the sad walk in the previous chapter—will go a long way toward defining the core personality that our character needs to express as he moves. The rest is subtle modification, albeit modification that is based on research, analysis, and reason beforehand.

Intrinsic Balance

Before we define our character by pose or gesture we should first have a clear understanding on how the average character should be constructed, based on known factors of balance and harmony within the anatomy. Clarification of this understanding was gleaned from a teaching colleague, Dr. Charles Wood, when we were discussing character design one day. To illustrate, I will use an orthographic (profile) shot of a generic character.

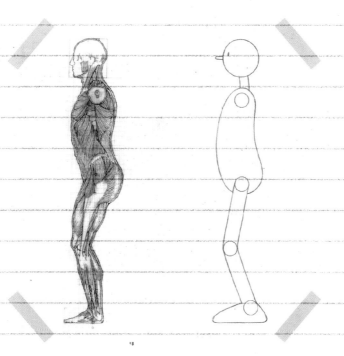

Central Balance

The first thing to understand is that a character's body will assume the pose of the best balance. Balance means that the muscles will work less and therefore we will achieve the greatest relaxation, and therefore the least strain and exhaustion. This being true we must first look at the most perfect balance line that will run through the entire body, from top to bottom.

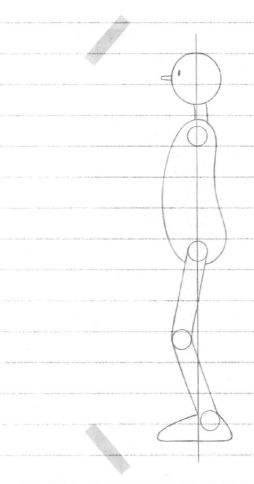

Note that all the parts of the body are pretty much set above one another, to create the perfect pose. Now we must consider the specific points in the body as they align themselves directly or indirectly under our central line of balance.

Center Point of Head

Generically, it might be said that the center point within the head is in front of the ear.

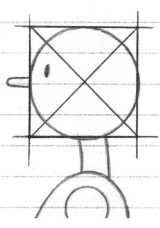

However, if the character design requires that the ear is consciously positioned higher or lower, toward the front or the back of the center position, it is possible to assess the head's center position by first blocking lines around the profile of the head and then drawing diagonals from each of the corners. The intersection of these will now establish the center point of the head.

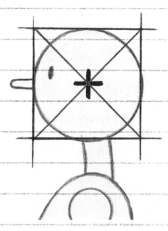

The key thing to remember is that once the center point of the head is known, it should be placed on the central balance line of the body.

Spine

The next thing to take into account is the spine. As we all know (or should know) the spine is essentially an S-curve, made up of individual vertebrae. The key point for our purposes is vertebrae T10, the 17th one down from the skull. This is the next point of alignment in our central line of balance.

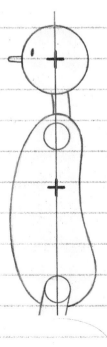

As long as the T10 point is directly below the center of the head in the central line of balance the character will be aligned in the most natural way possible.

Hips

The next point of alignment we must consider is that of the hips. If the character appears in perfect balance and alignment, then the hips need to be approximately beneath the head and spine points along that line of balance, however unconventional they may be.

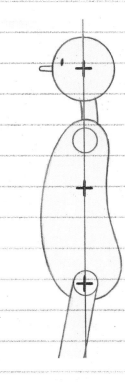

Knees and Feet

The final factors in our balanced pose concept are the knees and the feet. Here it is not so much a question of perfect alignment between the knees and feet since normally there is a slight bend to the knees, even in a perfectly upright stance. Consequently the knees may be just a little ahead of the line of balance. However, the arch of the foot, which is the point that can take the most pressure of weight exerted with downward force upon it, needs to be aligned on that balance line.

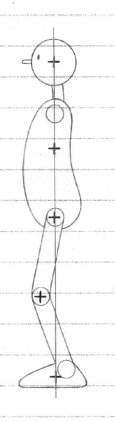

Knowing, therefore, what our character should look like in perfect balance we can adjust the pose in a way that best suits his personality. With the pose adjusted for that, we can animate his movement better and more accurately, hence the importance of establishing an ideal pose in the first place, usually initially defined in the turnaround model sheet of that character. For example, here is our character in a normal balanced pose.

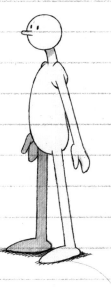

Now here is the same character when really angry.

Note how now there is a more aggressive lean forward with the much tenser muscles causing the posture to be tighter and more rigid looking. When we get angry we tend to do this. We tense our muscles, lean forward (i.e., getting more into the other person's face) and tend to move in a much more rigid fashion. On the website, you'll see how our character will walk generically.

And how that same character will walk when angry.

Note the more defined lean in the action, the shorter stride with a more stomping action, the clenched fists, the more assertive forward head position, and finally the more rigid and forward action of the arms. All this defines the mood or the personality of that person at that moment in time and is why it pays for an animator to consider the emotional condition of the character and how that affects the way he stands and moves.

Physical Limitations

Now let us look at a character whose physical limitations define her walk (on the website, www.animatorsnotebook.com) rather than her personality. To do this we will discuss a limping character. I have used this example before in my book, *How to Make Animated Films*, but it helps to express the challenges and the methods involved when animating a character who walks with physical limitations.

Environmental Adjustments

Often the environment will define just how a character will move. Starting with our generic character walk again … let us see how the same character's walk will be affected by the environment in which she is walking.

For example, if the character is walking into a strong wind her body lean (and to some extent the movement of her arms and legs) will be entirely different if she was walking into a strong wind or has that strong wind at her back. Walking into the wind demands that the body lean be far more forward, to gain the character more momentum when dealing with it. Here's what a normal body lean looks like, compared to one where the character is heading into the wind. It is likely too that the leg lift on the passing position will be lower, as that leg too will tend to be battling against the wind.

On the other hand, if the strong wind is at the character's back she will tend to lean more backward, to prevent herself from falling flat on her face with the wind pushing behind her. It might be likely too that the leg on the passing position is a little more forward of the midway location, because the strong wind will tend to force that free leg a little more forward as it moves through.

Similarly, for a character who is trying to walk uphill, again the body lean will need to be more extremely forward, as the character will be trying to get as much forward momentum as possible to get himself up the hill. However, on this occasion the passing position leg will tend to be higher and more forward since the character will need to get as much purchase on the ground as possible, and as soon as he possibly can, to ensure a more assured progress up the hill.

As with the example of the wind at the back, when walking down hill a character will tend to lean forward, to prevent it from being pitched forward down the hill. However, here the free leg of the passing position will tend to delay a little to ensure that the character has as much support as possible, for as long as possible, while leaning unnaturally backward.

Now let us give a practical example of a character performing a nongeneric walk. In this example we will take a character that is standing, carrying a long staff to support himself.

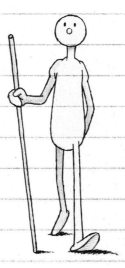

If we were to just add a staff and have the character do a basic walking action, the example you'll find on the companion website is what it would look like.

However, if we were to add a little pressure to the staff by having the character lean more of his weight onto the staff for support, then this is more what it would look like.

Note that the body lean is more pronounced to favor the staff side. This pose alone suggests that real weight is being applied to the staff as the character walks. Note too that here a little bit of limp is added to the action, meaning that the length of the stride on the free leg is a little longer than the stride on the staff side. This again emphasizes that the character is using the staff for support, giving a little more credibility to the action.

Now we need to bring a little more personality to the walk by having to consider the nature of the character walking in this way. For example, if the character was more of a depressed type, then the body language and the way the character moves with the staff will need to communicate this as he moves.

However, if the character is a more optimistic and playful type, we might have some fun with the action to give it more personality. For example, instead of the character taking two even strides as normal, what if he took two quick steps on the staff side to the one on the nonstaff side? Depending on how this was done it could be a quite amusing walk, defining much better the playful nature of the character.

See how that by just adding a little imagination to how we would normally move things we immediately bring more character, emotion, and personality to the movement? This is what accomplished animators must always try to do if they want to communicate more about the character they are animating to the watching audience. Yes, we all know how to make characters walk, and yes, if we add their individual design to a generic style walk it will somewhat identify their core identity. But if we begin to think beyond that and add individuality and change to their movement, too, in a way that entirely complements their emotional or character traits, then we indeed begin to bring out more personality in everything they do—in this case, the way they walk.

It goes without saying that in this day and age it is not always possible to go that extra few yards to achieve perfect personality action. However, if the action you are attempting requires that a little modification to the norm will enhance the scene, it does behoove you as a true character animator to make that extra effort and bring out of the character the underlying personality that is there. One look at the great action of the Disney animation from the distant past, or some of the Pixar animation that we see today, and you'll immediately see what defines personality from the purely generic.

Finally, let's look at some other peripheral tricks we might use to add elements of personality to a walk. For example, consider the way the head moves throughout the action. Normally we have the head upright and looking forward, with perhaps a little up-and-down movement if we are attempting to loosen up the action somewhat. However, what can we do to the head action to communicate personality?

Head Action

For a start, if our character is a happy-go-lucky type, try flicking the head from side to side as she walks. This gives a much jollier, more carefree sense to the action.

You can get an even more dramatic flick to this kind of head action if you delay the passing position location a little, to ensure it moves faster over the second part of the stride action than the first.

Neck and Shoulders

Simply by adjusting the positioning of the neck and shoulders you can communicate emotion and personality. For example, compare a more rigid, upright, and military-style attitude to the shoulder action, to that of a more slumped, sad, and depressed attitude.

Note too that the way the shoulders are set will significantly affect the way the arms will move over each stride. The perky, military-style action to the upper part of the body will reflect this in the way the arms move, whereas a sloping, slumped shoulder attitude will significantly incline the arms to drag or slide around the body more lethargically.

All this will more and more significantly define the personality nature of your character's way of moving.

Torso

The way the torso moves is a big indicator of personality. For example, our depressed, slumped shoulder character will much more likely have a curved inclination in the spine, as if the weight of the world was on his shoulders.

Alternatively, our more perky, military-style type will incline to a much more upright stance that communicates a much more positive, confident way of being.

Again, as with the perky head action, we can even add a side-to-side action to the body's movement, providing a definite strut to the more positive character—a delay at the passing position stage emphasizing the strutting action even more.

Remember your balance here, however! If you exaggerate the side-to-side lean on the body, you will have to adjust the whole character pose (especially from a front or back viewpoint) to ensure the body weight is over the point of contact and not beyond it.

Note that the center of gravity above is way beyond the two points of contact on the ground; therefore, it is unnaturally out of balance!

Legs

Even the leg action can define personality. The military-style guy will have a much more rigid, forward-and-back movement to the lower limbs. Everything will be straight, angular, and much more mechanical in its appearance. However, a typically depressed, lazy, or reluctant kind of character will quite literally tend to drag his feet as he walks, perhaps with the toes pointing inward on the passing position to emphasize his body language.

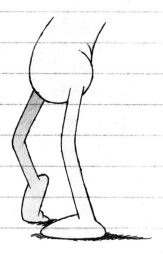

A little delay on the dragging foot in the passing position with some creative use of the timing/charting will tend to emphasize the dragging nature of the action, with a quick flip forward of the foot as it approaches the full stride hit position.

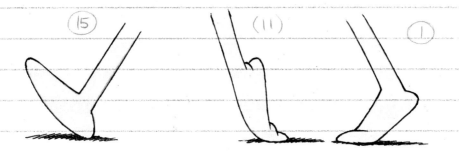

In Conclusion

These are just a few of the little tricks you can apply to your walking action to define attitude and personality. But these are only the tip of an iceberg of opportunity. Experiment yourself with this wide palette of options and see what you can come up with in defining personality in action.

Above all else—Observe Life!

By studying what real people—with real attitudes, emotions, and personality traits— do when they move you will begin to log in to your database of understanding real possibilities for your action. Look, film, sketch, and analyze. Do everything you can to understand just what defines one walk from another, one character's personality in movement from another. Shoot reference footage of yourself or a colleague acting out the extremes of the actions you have in mind and use this as key reference when you attempt to replicate this through your animation.

Remember, there are no shortcuts to great animation—even with the most user-friendly of animation software. You have to observe, try, iterate, and evolve your actions and not give up on them until you have fully achieved what you are going for.

Generic works generically. In other words, if you make it move you have technically animated it. But have you really brought it to life, with real character and personality, the way a great Pixar or old-Disney animator would do? If you have you will be within the ranks of the true character animators who can delight and make real for us the way a character is, drawing us into a world that we can empathize with and identify. If not, then you still have work to do! Hopefully all the material contained in this book will help you along that path of discovery and execution.

Suggested Assignment

Find a real person whose style of walking is individualistic and particularly appeals to you. Study, sketch, and film the way he or she walks, and then try to analyze and replicate it with an animated character of your choice. You may find that you will need to design a character that is more reflective of the person you are observing, but this would be a good exercise too.

For this assignment, remember that in designing a character—as indeed in animating that character—you will need to caricature reality, not just replicate it photographically.

Film and work over your animation several times until you arrive at the perfect interpretation of the character you have chosen.

chapter 5

Quadruped Walks

Perhaps the most difficult of all walks and the least talked about are quadruped walks. Here all the challenges of bipedal walks are intensified several-fold; not only is there another pair of legs to contend with, but the synchronization of those legs often varies from creature to creature, species to species. Additionally the size, weight, and bulk of that creature will be a factor in the way it walks. For example, a Gecko lizard will clearly walk very differently from a thoroughbred horse. A long and rangy giraffe will need to be approached in a very different way from that of a ground-hugging burrowing critter such as a mole. Add to the mix the fact that you also have to deal with head and tail movements—whether it's a cartoon-style quadruped or a naturalistic one—the enormity of the challenge is exponentially magnified!

Suffice it to say (and echoing the approach I took in my recent book, *How to Make Animated Films*) it would make much more sense to at least minimize the challenge by dealing with naturalistic-style quadrupeds and cartoon-style quadrupeds quite differently.

Naturalistic Quadrupeds

Before we get into details I would like to show an example of a quadruped that I once did for a TV commercial. The spot, for the British lager Lamot, required a very science-fantasy approach and consequently the beast that the hero rode upon did not exactly resemble anything in our known world, although it did somewhat follow the characteristics of a giant cat. To further complicate the matter the beast had to bear a warrior and descend a sand hill at the same time.

I researched a number of cats walking and made studies, both filmed and drawn. However, I was not able to reference a giant cat descending a sand hill with a rider on its back so I did the next best thing—a horse with a rider on its back descending a snowy hill! It was obviously a cold, snowy winter at the time so I was actually able to take advantage of the conditions. Luckily I found a willing rider who was prepared to take his horse down a snow-covered hill in Kent while I filmed the entire thing. The conditions were a little treacherous from the horse's point of view but we were at least able to capture the movement well, specifically the angle the horse positioned itself and the angle at which the rider was positioned to maintain balance while going downward on a sliding slope. Unfortunately I no longer have this reference footage to show; otherwise, I would show that too. Suffice it to say, several key pose positions emerged from that footage that I was later able to readjust in the form of the cat creature.

Naturalistic: Importance of Research

This example will underline the importance of research in animation. There is absolutely no way that I could have animated that scene without first having found out how cats walk and how any load-bearing quadruped would walk downhill with a weight on its back. This does not apply to quadrupeds only. The message is again and again, with animation, that research is the first stage of any animation process, especially directly from nature wherever possible. Study your subject matter, and then plan how you can execute it through the character and the medium in which you are working. The process and form of animation you use after that are your choice. However, and the need to study and research your subject beforehand is paramount to all animators in every style.

Naturalistic: Breaking Down the Action

It may be possible for other animators to work on the whole character at once but I find it best to break the design down into units that I can handle in an easier way. Consequently, I will use another cat example I featured elsewhere in one of my books to clarify this process. Here's the original cat design sketch that I initially received from my close colleague, Dr. Charles Wood.

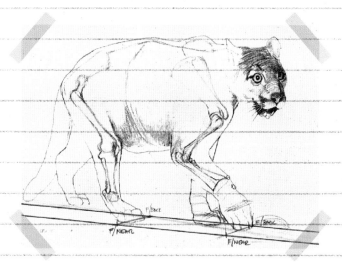

Clearly there is a lot to consider here. So before animating it I broke the design down into easily moveable parts. I will use traditional hand-drawn 2D animation to illustrate this process but there is no reason why 3D, or other forms of animation, cannot use this process to achieve their objectives too. Note how I have separated the front legs with the back legs to animate both in their own right and separately.

I've broken the broad anatomy of the character into quite simple geometric shapes, making their movement as easy as possible.

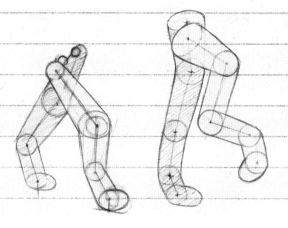

From such individual parts it is far easier to focus on specific parts of the quadruped action in question. So, study the reference action you have of your chosen animal over and over again and begin to analyze specifically the sections of its movement you are dealing with at the time.

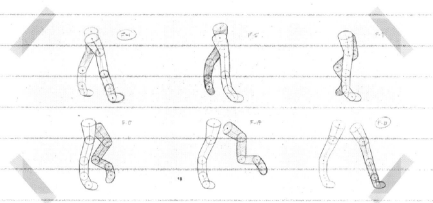

Then take the element you want to deal with first and work with it on its own (and on its own layer if you're specifically working in traditional 2D animation). For the purposes of illustration, let's take the front legs first. Here is my action for the front legs of the puma.

And the example on the website is what it looks like when animated.

Note how a cat places its feet down claw first, as opposed to heel first as with human characters. Remember too that all the basic principles that applied to generic walks in Chapter 2 apply here, especially the concept of the body rising on the passing position.

Having completed the required action with the front legs I will then move to the back legs and animate them as their own walk action. Note with the anatomy of any realistic quadruped that the action of the back legs is not identical to the front. Therefore, you will have to return to your reference footage again and analyze just how they work with the particular animal you are animating. Here's what the back legs of my creature look like in sequence.

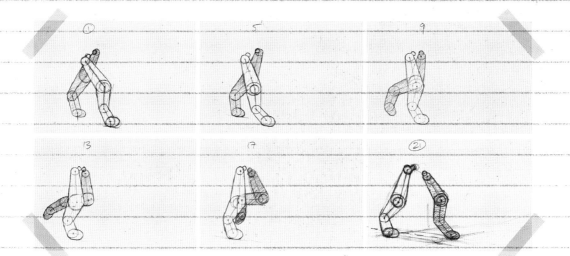

And the next example is what they look like when moving.

With the front and back legs completed we can now consider the rest of the body's action, which again can be taken in stages. First we need to consider the basic body action that links the two pairs of legs, so first position the legs as far apart as they need to be, and then add the body linking them.

Study your reference footage and note how the mass of the body moves in unison with the legs. Note the synchronization of the legs first, however, to ascertain the sequence in which your particular animal places its feet down. It invariably will not place the lead front foot down at the same time as the back legs, so you have to observe the sequence used and adjust your front legs/back legs action accordingly.

With the synchronization of the legs established you should then apply the movement of the body connecting them and how the leg actions affect the movement of the masses in the body that links them. Think too of the kind of musculature that the body contains, referencing any anatomical material you can find that helps you better understand exactly what tissue and muscle groups are moving under the skin. Take into consideration also the effect of gravity on the weight of the body mass and the degree to which the body sags between the front and back legs. Referencing the original material is always recommended.

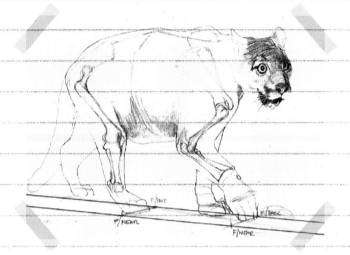

With the body movement established and successfully linking the leg movements it is time to consider the neck and head action. Again, remember the overlapping action principles that we employed in the generic walk discussion earlier, especially with regard to the head. (i.e., as the body moves up the head tends to remain down a little and when the body moves down the head tends to remain somewhat up). We can apply this somewhat to the action of the head, but only inasmuch as the reference material we are using from reality confirms what we are trying to attempt.

Remember too that whenever tackling reality—in the sense that our animation should look real and not cartoonish—we are not just precisely copying the real action but are actually caricaturing it! That means that although our animated character has to conform entirely to the realistic world, we do need to push it further than displayed in our filmed footage of the real key positions to that when seen in a virtual, CG, or other world.

Remember

Animated reality looks dead and flat if it's just traced or mo-capped at face value—it will only look real if taken beyond what is real in the physical world!

Consequently, when animating a quadruped the animator needs to consider two main actions at this stage, the head action and the neck action. Broadly stated, when the front legs push that part of the body upward, the neck connected to that body would tend to hold back down a little, to create the overlapping action effect. However, with regard to the head action, it is when the neck is moving upward that the head will drag a little behind it in staying down, and then again when the neck is moving down the head will stay up a little longer in compensation. That way there will be a double overlapping action effect, the degree of application depending entirely on the nature of the creature being animated and the length and suppleness of the joints and masses being moved.

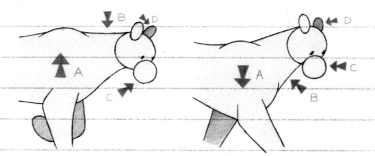

Now all that remains is the addition of a tail (assuming the creature being animated has a tail). The extremeness of this action will again depend on the length and flexibility of the tail being studied. But generically it should be recognized that the same principles of overlapping action that appear on the neck and head are reflected here, although it is best to consider for the purposes of smoothness and flexibility that the tail has a huge number of joints all reacting to each other whereas the head and neck are just two.

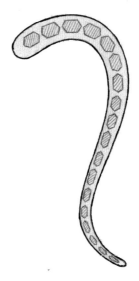

We will approach this tutorial as if the tail is long and flexible, so that the animator will have to scale-down the following if the tail he or she is working on is shorter and more rigid.

Remember that the overlapping effect we discussed in the head and neck action was effectively a short successive breaking of joints (a process discussed in Chapter 11). With the head and neck, the neck's action is entirely dependent on the body's action while the head's action is dependent on the neck's movement; similarly with the tail, albeit many times more!

Remember too that the root of the tail is connected to the body of the animal at the rump. Consequently the root will be affected by the movement of the rump and every imagined joint beyond that affected by the one ahead of it. As the root moves up the imagined joints of the tail will follow it, although each one will delay slightly behind the one ahead of it in the chain. Therefore, when the tail is animating up and down in accordance with the body, then the flowing wave-like action of the tail will tend to look like the example you'll find on the website.

Remember, however, that the root of the tail is always subject to the movement of the rump of the animal in question, so since there will be a forward and back rotation to the hips of the back legs (as also discussed in the generic walks section) the tail will not just be rippling up and down but also side to side! This means that the animation of the tail will be entirely dependent for its action on the physical nature of the animal in question, the length and flexibility of its limbs and movement, and that degree to which it rotates the hip section of its rump. Consequently, achieving a believable tail action on some creatures is the hardest challenge an animator might face in moving a quadruped (especially if animating a cat and the cat is independently flapping its tail when it is angry!).

That said, if a quadruped's action is approached in sections as we just indicated, then it should make the animator's task considerably more accessible. Now let us look at the animation process for creating a purely cartoon-style quadruped, which should make understanding all of this much easier.

Cartoon Style

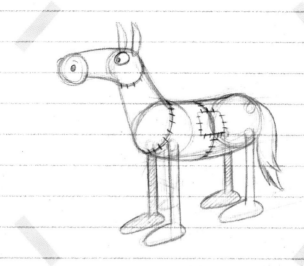

When approaching the animation of a more traditional, pantomime cartoon horse we begin in exactly the same way. We need to break down all the elements of the horse design into separate elements: front legs, back legs, torso, head, neck, and tail. With these elements more clearly defined it will make our task all the easier.

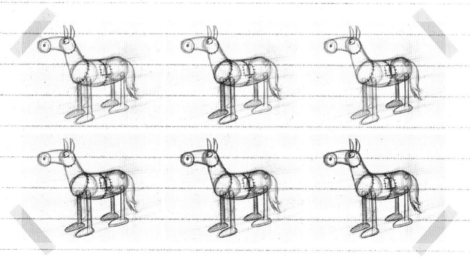

Remember that with the legs separate and the horse being entirely cartoon in nature we can do anything with its movement; that is, we're not limited to replicating reality. Indeed, depending on the nature of the production in which the animated horse will appear, we can become quite outlandish in the way we make it move.

To illustrate this point I am going to make the movement on the front legs entirely different from that on the back, with the rest of the body fitting in to the action as best as it can. Consequently we will simply focus on one pair of legs to start with, although we must remember that the foot slide (see Chapter 2) on both pairs of legs has to remain identical if the illusion of unity between all the four legs is to be maintained (and one pair of feet is not apparently slipping along with the others). In the following case we will start with the front legs.

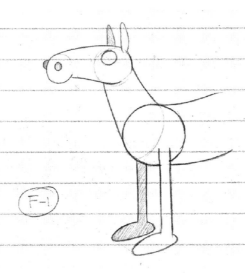

For this exercise we will animate the action on two's, although if you want to ultimately put it on one's it will appear much smoother. First, the front legs need to be positioned in all the key stride positions. This will give us the positioning and range of the strides these legs will take.

It might be a good idea to define the stride positions of the back legs at this point, so that you don't find they cross each other or get in each other's way later.

With the stride positions in place for the front legs, next establish the passing position.

With these in place, it is time to put in the in-betweens. These can be quite eccentric in nature because we want this pantomime character to move in quite unorthodox ways. However, they still need to confirm to all the principles of biped action we defined in Chapter 2. You'll find an example on the website of what it looks like when animated.

With the front legs complete, we should now turn to the back legs. Remember to locate these exactly in the same position, since they need to appear for the finished horse action. Hopefully by now you will have established the key stride positions and they will not in any way be conflicting with the movement you have created for the front legs.

Again add the passing positions to this action, remembering that in this particular case the back leg action will not be the same as the front leg action. Therefore, these passing positions will be very different from each other.

(F-19)

(S-25)

Now add the in-betweens to the back legs, which like the passing position will be very different from the ones used for the front legs.

Now check out how this action looks when animated on the website.

With both sets of legs in place it is now time to add the body. Remember that even in a cartoon world there has to be some consistency. The great Walt Disney used to talk of "plausible implausibility" in his time, meaning that although the world of animation was often implausible in comparison with the real world, it nevertheless had to conform to its own laws of weight, gravity, mass, shape consistency, and so on if the audience was going to buy into what was being shown to them. Consequently, with the body of our horse it is very important that we maintain some consistency of shape and volume if we are to convince the audience that our horse is real, even though it's clearly a cartoon horse. So, when the lines of the body are added to connect to the two sets of legs the squashing and stretching that will ensue must consistently maintain the essential volumes that the body has. Here are some extremes of the body shapes that link the legs at different stages of the walk.

T-23

On the website, you'll find an example of what it looks like when animated on its own level.

With the body successfully added to the legs it is time now to consider the head. As with the realistic horse earlier we need to consider the head and the neck as separate overlapping elements that are attached to the front legs. Chapter 11 will explain in detail how the notion of successive breaking of joints works but for now let's just accept that each joint moves independently of each other and each moves as a result of the one that is moving higher in the chain. In this case I am considering three joints to complete our movement—the neck joint, the jaw joint, and a joint that links the ears to the head.

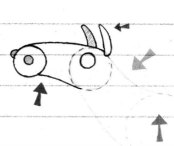

We will follow precisely the same principle of overlapping movement we applied to the realistic quadruped earlier, only this time we will exaggerate them further since this is a cartoon character and therefore needs to be more expressive and exaggerated in its movement. So, first taking the neck, let us remind ourselves of the rule that as the body rises, the neck will drag back a little.

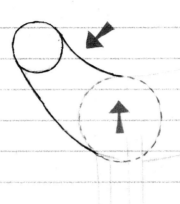

Following the successful movement of the neck, we should now remember that as the neck rises, the head would slightly delay behind it and vice versa when it descends.

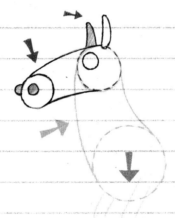

Finally, since we are animating even the ears on our cartoon character, we need to establish that as the head moves up and down (or forward and back perhaps) the ears will tend to drag behind it as it goes.

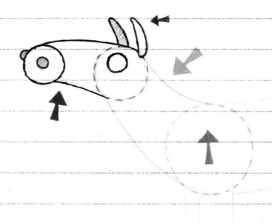

Putting everything together we arrive at a fluid head and neck action.

Finally we turn to the tail to complete our pantomime horse action. Everything we said about the tail in the realistic quadruped applies here, but again even more so since it is a cartoon action, not a realistic one. So there will be much more fluid whiplash appearing in the action as the tail responds to the body moving up and down with the leg action. On the next page there are some typical stages of the tail flipping as the back of the body moves.

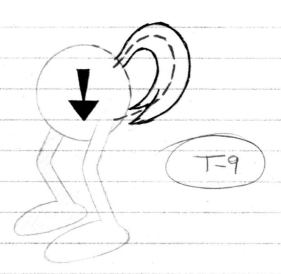

Remember that for the tail we are essentially dealing with a cracking whip action in the most extreme cases. So like a cracking whip, the more fluid tail will follow the action of the driving force of the rear as it moves up or down. This is often described as overlapping or secondary animation.

To understand the tail/whip action more clearly, it might help to think of any fluid shape like a tail, a whip, or even a flag as being a curved and flexible shape sandwiched between a series of rollers.

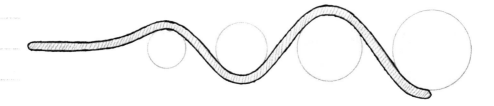

As the rollers move the fluid shape will transform to their contours, effectively giving the action we are requiring for the tail or other similar objects to be animated.

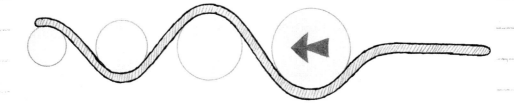

On the website is another very simple example of a flicking tail when you use the principle of fluid overlapping action to get a sense of a whip.

Remember that all these examples are just the tip of the iceberg of possibilities. The options are infinite when putting a cartoon quadruped action together. Different leg actions; different and more varied head, neck, and tail actions; and indeed even a different character design will ensure that your animation will look far different from mine. Remember too the personality and the eccentricity we talk about in other notebook tutorials, which—like the mood, terrain, and environmental conditions imposed on the character—will show that the way a quadruped walks is infinite in its expression and limited only by your own imagination!

Suggested Assignment

Depending on your interest, I would suggest that in order to test yourself on the knowledge contained in this tutorial you attempt one (or both) of the following tutorials. The following assignments are taken from my book, *How to Make Animated Films* (Focal Press).

1. Realistic quadruped: Take the reference footage provided in the book's companion website (or from a definitive movie clip of a quadruped of your own choice) and create a realistic quadruped action based upon it. Film your action, repeating it FIVE times.

2. Cartoon quadruped: Taking a three-quarter view of the pantomime horse design illustrated in the book, and create a cycle of it walking eccentrically (i.e., the front legs and the back legs should feature a different style of walk movement) but differently from the version I have illustrated in this chapter. Film your final walk, repeating it five times.

chapter 6

Generic Runs

Now that we have dealt with generic walks, eccentric walks, and personality walks in other tutorials in this book, it is time to focus our attention on generic runs. There really is no one tutorial on runs that encompasses everything, since effectively every run is unique to itself. None can be strictly described as generic, but there are core principles of runs that enable the action to be discussed more generically, after which some further sophistication can be added to the basics.

Misconceptions About Runs

It is often wrongly assumed by many novice animators that a run is merely a faster version of a walk. Nothing could be farther from the truth! If you look carefully at a run in slow motion you will note one major difference between a run and a walk. With a run *both* feet come off the ground at a certain part in the action, whereas with a walk one foot is always in contact with the ground at any moment in time. Indeed, this is the definition of a run put out by all the race walking associations—that a walk becomes a run (and is therefore disqualified) if both feet do indeed come off the ground at the same time!

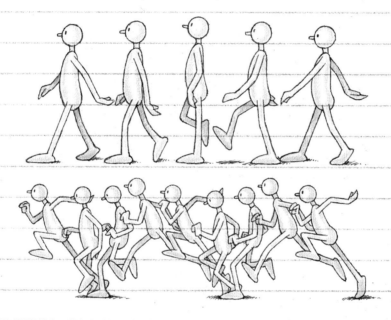

Therefore, a run is more of a controlled jump than a speeded-up walk, where the character in question changes from leg to leg in the process. To clarify this let us introduce ourselves to the five key positions of a generic run.

Drive Off

To get a really convincing running action we first have to start with a good drive-off position. Of course the more powerful the running action is the more dynamic the drive-off position has to be. However, the essential elements of the drive off are that the contact leg is pushing the body firmly forward and the lead leg is held up and forward in anticipation of the stride itself.

Remember too that with any Olympic-level sprinter, it is the arms that drive the legs faster. Therefore, the more powerful and dynamic the arms are, the more convincing the drive-off position will be.

Stride Position

With a good drive-off position realized the character now has to achieve a strong transition pose position before hitting the landing on the other foot. This is known as the stride position. Here the body already has been driven up and forward by the rear leg and so the entire body is now off the ground, legs separated. The faster the run the wider the stride that needs to be achieved here. Again, an Olympic sprinter will have an enormous distance of the stride position whereas a marathon runner, for example, will have a very small stride. Physically what is going on with the stride position is that the leg that has already driven off is dragging behind, whereas the foot that was rising up at the drive-off position is now reaching forward to prepare for touch down at the next contact point.

Leg Reach Down

The third position we need to consider with a walk is the leg reach down. This is effectively where the leg that has been leading on the stride position now reaches down and makes its initial contact with the ground. It is true to say that there is effectively nothing like a passing position in a run. However, this pose is the closest thing to it. For example, with one leg touching the ground the free leg is moving forward, about to come through and reach its midway position to what would be the generic passing position of a walk. The arms at this stage would be in a more downward position, close to the body and about swap position as the stride changes.

Contact/Squash Position

Now, with the lead foot firmly fixed to the ground the body drops down into a squash position, as a result of the body mass and momentum exerting a great deal of pressure on it. The contact leg therefore is bent to absorb this shock while the free leg is swinging through (to prepare for its next drive position).

The squash of course depends a lot on the size and weight of the character doing the running—a heavier character has more impact on the legs than a light one.

Drive-Off

Again we are back to the original drive-off position, albeit this time the opposite foot is on the ground and the other leg is driving up and forward. This effectively completes the first stride cycle and starts the second one.

Body Angle

I have discussed elsewhere the fact that all biped movement, walks or runs, requires a certain amount of body lean to initiate momentum. The more the character's body leans the faster the action must be. Consequently, the body lean of a run needs to be far more exaggerated than that of a walk, except perhaps of a run that is more closely aligned to a marathon run than a sprint, in which case there needs to be an economy of action both in terms of momentum and even arm action. However, within the lean it requires a variation within each stride that will tend to make the action more natural and convincing, for example, if we establish the body lean of a character in the drive position as the following.

Note that the lean is quite pronounced. However, at the point where the lead leg is reaching down and touching the ground, the body lean will need to be farther back somewhat as the leg extension will tend to rotate the upper body backward slightly.

The other stride positions will therefore have variations to the original drive position angle, perhaps as so:

This will only emphasize the action of the run, making it more dynamic and believable. Clearly, however, this works best with dynamic runs, where there is a wider range of action than, say, with a slow, marathon-style runner.

Arm Actions

Another way of giving more identity to the run is to vary the way the arms move. For example, with a more sprinting action the usual pendulum-style pumping action will work fine.

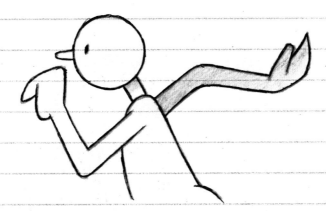

However, in a more desperate, struggling kind of run you might consider the arms moving differently. In this example they are moving through an oval path of action, slightly emulating a swimming action or an action where the arms are seemingly grasping at air to try and pull themselves forward in addition to the dynamic leg drive.

Another variation would be a stiffer and more limited straight-arm style, where the arms are left pretty much straight and the action is more like fast pendulums than bent, pumping sprinter's arms.

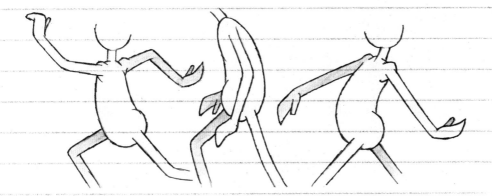

The shape and action of the arms will very much define the personality or emotional need of the running action.

3-Frame Run

The 3-frame run is a traditional "scrabbling-style" run that was often used in the older style form of animation. This was often used as much for economy purposes than for its emotional content, since these were used mostly in TV animation and low-budget shorts.

The 3-frame run
- The drive off
- The stride
- The squash landing

As its name suggests, the 3-frame run basically breaks down the stride action into three key leg positions, the minimum possible to describe a running action. The effect creates an almost blurred, scrabble style of run. The three positions are

The drive off: This is pretty much the same as our standard run position for the drive off, with contact leg straight and pushing the body forward and the lead knee bent and forward.

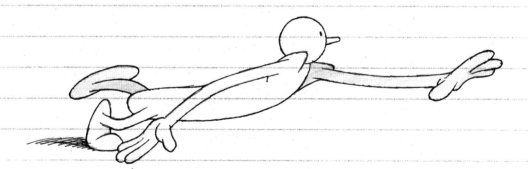

The stride: Again, pretty much the same as the conventional stride position but perhaps with the legs even farther apart than normal.

The squash landing: This is a kind of combination between the contact pose and the squash before the push-off pose. The lower you make this pose (and the higher you make the stride pose) the more "up and down" there is to the action.

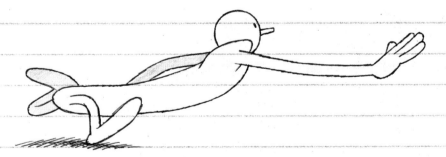

It is worth repeating here that the 3-frame run is the minimum possible to get the sense of a character running, and therefore it is a more stylistic cartoon approach than a naturalistic one. Go to the website for a sample of this kind of run that I used for an aggressive black swan action.

Keys Only

It is clear from the above that a run stride is essentially five separate key poses that, unlike a walk, really do not offer any opportunities for conventional in-betweens. In a traditionally drawn animation world these key positions would be shot on two's (i.e., one drawing for two frames). However, a good exercise for every animator is to consider adding in-between positions to all the five key poses to create a greater sense of naturalness and smoothness. You will of course also need to create all the positions of a stride on the other leg, too, so that the entire run cycle action is complete.

Run Cycles Versus Straight Ahead Action

As with repeated actions like walks and runs, it is natural for most animators to want to create a repeat action and to use it over and over again.

Although you can probably get away with this a few times, if you use the repeat effect more than that the audience will notice it and will not be inspired by what you do. Consequently, it is preferable (if you have the time or budget) to animate your action straight ahead with each stride, meaning that you repeat nothing and create every stride as new activity. This can be unnecessary if a robotic, mechanical feel is required for a character's action. However, if you want to put surprise, personality, and unpredictability into the action you will be far better off using this kind of straight ahead technique, especially if you're creating a personality run.

Foot Slide and Background Panning Speed

When a cycle action is created for either a walk or a run the character effectively moves on the spot with the background or environment moving past at exactly the same speed as the contact foot slides on the ground. This is best illustrated by showing the foot on a walk cycle moving back, as an identifiable part of the background near the foot moves in perfect synchronization with it.

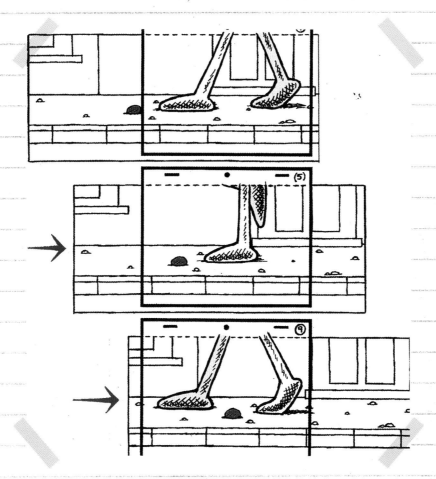

If the background or environment is moving faster or slower than the foot slide, then the character will appear to be slipping, as if walking on ice.

Slow-Motion Runs

Naturalistic runs, in accordance with the true laws of nature, can never be too slow. As we stated earlier, a run is defined as an action of motion that has both feet off the ground at a moment in time. Therefore, in the real world, a character cannot possibly hang in the air during the stride position forever. However, to give the illusion of this happening in the CG or animation world we have to explore the properties of slow motion. It is perfectly possible to slow down a run to infinite proportions of speed by just adding in-betweens.

However, remember that if something is moving extremely slowly, every facet of its pose and motion will be much more open to scrutiny. Even if the core motion is solid you will find that it benefits you to add additional touches of detail, such as extreme overlapping action and additional (normally unseen) features such as saliva flowing from the mouth or the chest widening and closing in a way that suggests extreme breathlessness. Similarly the character will blink extremely slowly, giving all kinds of possibilities of having fun with the eyes and eyelids. At the same time, a long-distance marathon runner will definitely move at a much slower speed than a sprinter. So that action will again be open to much more scrutiny than will the action of a fast run, such as a sprinter's.

Never Neglect Your Research

The bottom line with all these things, however, is research, research, and even more research! Always go to life and nature for your first point of reference, never the work of others, if you can. Even the finest animation in the world had to start somewhere and the odds are that the animation is the finest because it emanated first from an intense study of natural action. The closer you can emulate the action of the real world, however much it is extended and caricatured, the more chance that you will animate that action perfectly. This is especially true when you are attempting slow runs or even slow-motion runs.

Pose Is Everything

However, remember that if you are seeking to recreate the more naturalistic (but slow) action of a marathon runner the pose and stride of the action will be very different from that of a natural running action recreated in slow motion. Long-distance running requires that the character maintains his or her reserves of energy for the longer haul; therefore, the stride has to be shorter, the up-and-down action less, and the dynamic arm action reduced. Alternatively, a sprinter seen in slow motion will still have an extreme extended stride, a powerful punching action to the arms, and a more extreme up-and-down body lean as the run. Again, it is all a question of examining real life and then adapting it to the requirements of the action needed in front of you.

Reminder on Stride Length

Don't forget that the more power that is put into a run the more the stride length must be. The length of stride for a sprinter or 200- and 400-meter runner is far greater than that of a long-distance or marathon runner. Similarly, the length of stride in a walk will be far less than the stride length of a run.

Environmental Issues

The terrain and environment of running characters will also affect the way they move (true for walks too!). For example, if a character is running up a hill, his body lean and arm/leg action will be modified to enable him to ascend the incline successfully. This means that he will need a more pronounced lean to the body action and the arms will have to pump even harder to get the legs going.

On the other hand, if the character is running down a hill, his body language will be the opposite, meaning he will tend to lean backward more and adjust his foot and leg positioning as brakes to prevent him from tumbling head over foot downward. The arms will also be adjusted accordingly.

Head-on Runs

Living in a 3D world animators today must consider approaching their run (or any other animation for that matter) from all viewpoints. Even if the camera position is fixed it doesn't hurt to check and style your action from all angles; although it may not be seen in different angles it will actually work better for the audience if it does work from every viewpoint. To go partway toward this, let us consider animating a run head on.

The major thing to think of when animating a running action in anything but a profile viewpoint is the fact that the body weight doesn't just shift from side to side—it also shifts from one foot to another. This means that if the character has its right foot on the ground, its weight will shift across slightly to that right leg and vice versa when the left leg is down.

The amount of weight transfer will vary according to the kind of run being attempted and the nature of the character doing it. For example, a heavy character doing a slow, lumbering run will tend to shift from one side to the other more than a thin, light character running like a bullet.

Another factor that traditional (hand-drawing) animators should take into consideration is the exaggerated use of perspective in their drawings. This means that the parts of the body that are nearest the camera will tend to appear much larger, while those far away will tend to appear much smaller.

Suggested Assignment

Sometimes it is good to attempt a suggested assignment to enable all this information to process in your mind. Therefore, the following is a suggestion that will enable you to get a running action under your belt. (It's a toughy though!)

Take a character of your choice and have it either run around a circular course, linking up to its first position, or else just have it running on a cycle and rotate the camera around it in a 360-degree tracking action. This will not only enable you to create a basic running action using a cycled movement; it will also force you to consider the action from all angles, ensuring that you thoroughly understand what is going on with the character and its movement from every angle. I once did a similar exercise for an exaggerated, eccentric walking action. See the website for an example.

This is, of course, especially challenging for traditional animators where every drawn pose has to be carefully considered.

All animators attempting to animate the running around a circular course should remember that there would be a certain amount of inward lean required to the turn to make it entirely convincing (i.e., like a motorcyclist leaning inward to negotiate a tight corner).

chapter 7

Jumps

This chapter deals primarily with the process of animating jumps, or indeed anything that actively challenges the force of gravity. The effects of gravity, such as weight, will feature strongly in the other tutorials, but our interest here is focused mainly on the issues relating to a character launching himself upward, against gravity, seeking to leave the ground, and then returning earthward under the force of gravity once again. All jumps are underpinned by the basic principles of the bouncing ball, so first we'll remind ourselves of the most widely used and acknowledged principle for introducing animation to first-time students.

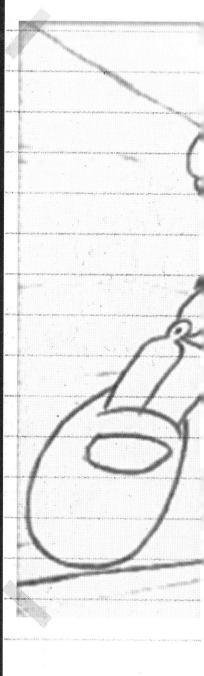

Bouncing Ball

The bouncing ball principle varies in accordance with the nature of the ball that is being bounced; here we will approach the principle using a standard rubber ball.

For further information on the bounding ball principle, refer to my previous books, From Pencils to Pixels: Classical Technique for Digital Animators and How to Make Animated Films, both from Focal Press.

To make things easier, we'll just look at the two key bounce positions first and then the passing position and in-betweens.

The upper of the two key positions will look like this:

The lower position will be like this:

See how the ball in the upper key position is perfectly round in shape, but when it is in the contact key position on the ground, it is deformed to reflect the squash position created as its pliable mass hits the solid ground.

Now see how the chart placements of the in-betweens will reveal that this is not a mechanical action but one that requires you to create a specific, convincing effect as the ball bounces. A typical slow-in/slow-out chart defines the kind of action that will link the upper positions to the lower positions of the bounce. (Note: The chart 11 through 21 represents the upward rise of the ball to its uppermost position and the chart 1 through 11 represents its movement from the apex position back down to the ground again.)

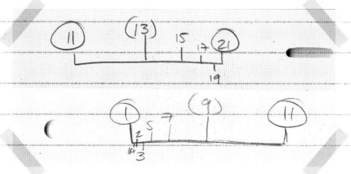

Let's see this slow-in/slow-out action visually.

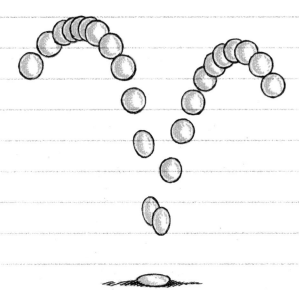

Try to remember what happens when you throw a rubber ball into the air. When it leaves your hand, it is at its fastest. But as it goes higher it tends to slow as a combination of air resistance and the force of gravity pull on it. Then, as it reaches the apex of its arc upward, it slows significantly to a point where it is almost stopped. That is why there is a slow-in and slow-out to and from the upper of the two keys.

From the upper movement the ball instantaneously returns to earth—very slowly at first, but then increasingly fast as the forces of gravity pull it down faster and faster. When the ball hits the ground it immediately flattens, then bounces straight up again in the same fashion, although this time the height will be less at the apex as its momentum is reduced by the impact of its collision with the earth. It will then continue with a reduced bounce in the very same fashion, and so on through a series of reducing bounces until it finally comes to a halt on the ground at the very end.

Go to the website to see what our animated ball will look like when it is moving.

You will see from the action that just like a regular thrown ball, this animated ball has a fast, snappy effect when hitting the ground and bouncing upward again—but its shape is significantly distorted as it is pulled down or stretches against gravity during its trajectory. Note too that the ball will slow to a stop at the top of its bounce and start to accelerate as it begins its downward path.

Let's look again at the kind of movement that's happening here, using superimposed placements of each frame.

Remember again that the more frames there are in an action, the slower that action will be. That is why we put a slow-in and a slow-out at the top of the bouncing ball's arc, to ensure that it will decelerate as it approaches the apex and then accelerate as it passes it. This is all textbook stuff when it comes to the use of slow-ins and slow-outs and something we should always bear in mind when we consider animating a jumping character in action.

Note too the distorted "stretch" of the ball as it reaches the breakdown positions of its actions, both on the way up and on the way down. Often the stretch position of the ball on its way down can be slightly more exaggerated because the ball will tend to move faster under the force of gravity than with it. It is also advised that the first ball position beyond the "squash" position is actually moved away from a contact with the ground, otherwise the ball will tend to stick on the ground a little too much when moving. Unless this is the effect desired, as illustrated here.

The stretched shape of the ball is a traditional animator's way of describing the kind of blur you would see if you film a real ball moving fast downward when you freeze a frame of live-action film.

Note too that as the ball arrives at the top of its arc, at the apex of the bounce its shape will tend to deform back to the perfectly round shape before descending again and therefore deforming into its more stretched shape.

Comparing Bouncing Balls of Different Types

So far we have concerned ourselves with just a standard rubber ball bounce. Now let's briefly compare this action with the bounce of balls of differing structure and mass.

Remember that balls will bounce entirely in accordance with the nature and content of their construction. Consequently, a ping-pong ball and a cannonball will bounce entirely differently from a standard rubber ball. The ping-pong ball, being light and very bouncy, will tend to bounce much higher due to its springiness, with a greater slowing-in and slowing-out to and from the apex of its upper arc. A cannonball, on the other hand, will barely leave the ground after its first bounce, due to its dense mass, weight, and lack of springiness. Here is a comparison of how the three different kinds of balls might look when placed side by side, from light to heavy.

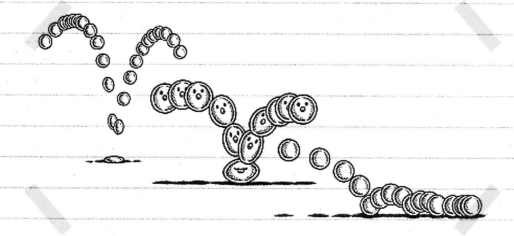

Now let's return to our jumping character action.

The Standing Jump

Just as we did with the bouncing ball, we'll start by discussing a character jumping up and down again on the spot. Here is our character.

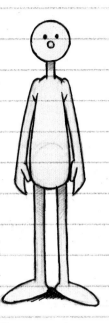

Remember that in anything we plan to animate, gravity will always exert an influence. Just as the ascent of the ball is decelerated by the force of gravity and its descent is accelerated, so too will gravity affect the way we move our jumping character—unless, of course, we are dealing with the world of the Warner Brothers-style characters who seem to walk off the edge of sheer cliff faces and stand on thin air until they realize their error. (After which gravity will again exert a force, of course!) This is one of animation's great traditions.

Another is the principle of **anticipation**, to which we will devote a whole notebook tutorial elsewhere, but for now let's just suggest that before we move a character in a particular line of force, it first benefits us to have a little anticipation of that character before we do so. This traditionally means that if a character is going to run off to the right side of the screen, if we have them make some kind of small move in the opposite direction first, it will give the entire action a greater sense of force and believability.

Consequently, if we want a character to jump upward, it will benefit us to have that character anticipate this move by dropping down a little before he takes off—something like this.

We will get more impact in our anticipation if we put a small slow-in to the downward pose. Here's how an animation chart would describe this move.

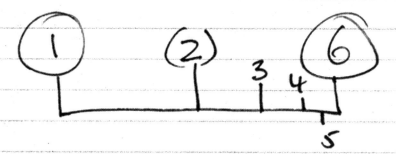

And here's what the action positions would look like.

Following our brief anticipation, we now need to have the character jump to the highest possible position in the air. Remember to keep this within the bounds of reasonable believability—although technically with animation we can do anything we like, of course. However, to once again quote Walt Disney's famous phrase—plausible implausibility—we need to make what we do within that world as plausible as possible to that world. This would naturally change if we were deliberately stretching reality, like the Warner Brothers characters and the cliff. Consequently, I suggest the following poses as being plausible to our jump action.

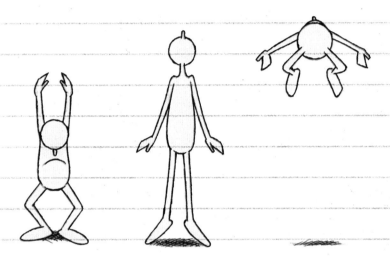

Now, referring to our bouncing ball principle of the movement slowing-in to the upper part, we should do the same with our animated character jump. Here's a suggestion for the in-between chart.

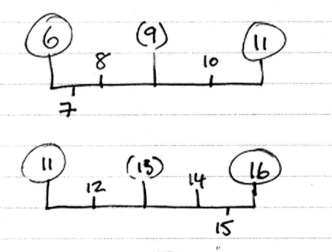

And here's what the action positions would look like using that chart.

It pays us to repeat the fact that the more frames there are in an action, the slower that action will be. Consequently, with all our drawings bunched to the top of the action, it will tend to slow it down there.

Now, having reached the maximum height with our character's jump, we need to bring it down to earth again. We again follow the principles of the bouncing ball to do this. First create the beginning and end poses of the action. Of course, the beginning pose is the one we've already used for the jump upward, but the ground contact one will need to look something like the following.

Again, as with the bouncing ball, we will need a slowing-out from the top position as the character moves down to the contact position.

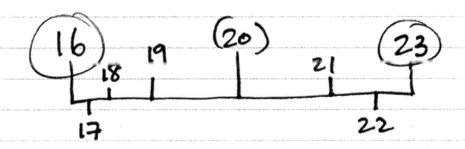

This will give us action frames something like this.

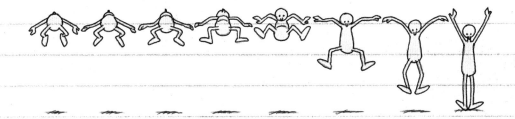

In actual fact, the landing of the character will need two poses to be created. The first, as we have seen, is where the feet first touch the ground.

However, we now need to create a second key that shows the "give" in the legs as the character's weight and velocity exert an effect on the contact legs. Do a short jump off a chair and see for yourself. When our legs touch the ground after a jump, they don't just stop and hold our body there. They have to give a little under the weight, much like the shock absorbers in a car take the impact as the car hits a bump in the road. Consequently, our knees will bend to take the impact as we attempt to absorb the weight of our bodies coming down. Therefore, our impact pose after the jump hit will look something like this.

Also, to give the action a greater sense of weight and resistance in the legs, I suggest a slowing-in of the action, charted something like this.

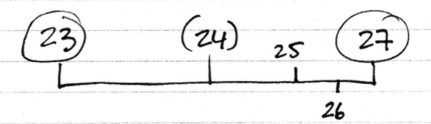

This will give us action poses like this.

Having sunk to the lowest cushioning position necessary, we now need to bring the character to our initial still and upright position again.

I again suggest a slowing-in action to give a smoothness to the upright return, perhaps charted something like the following.

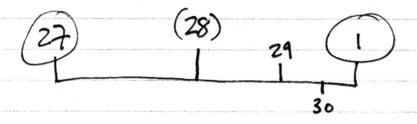

This gives us action poses like these.

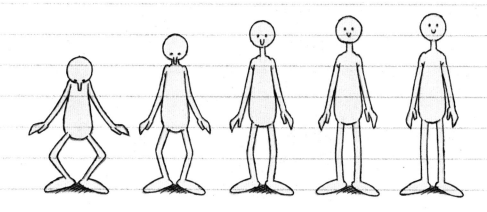

Finally, piecing all this together, we get an action something like the example you can see on the website.

You might notice one little thing we haven't talked about. In doing a down anticipation at the beginning, I actually animated a slight upward anticipation to the downward one before it happens. This kind of double anticipation can give an even more believable action than if you just do a simple single one. I think it tends to work better this way. Yes?

The Running Jump

So far, all our action examples in this tutorial have been produced with a character jumping up and down on the spot. However, most animation will not be like this, so now we should examine how to put a jump on the end of a character's run. This is somewhat like what field athletes do when they attempt a long jump event in track and field.

First we need to start the action with a fast character run. We dealt with character runs in Chapter 6 so there is no need to cover that ground here. Suffice it to say, the run should appear dynamic and consistent and definitely provide enough momentum on the character to ensure a strong forward motion when she attempts to jump.

Next we need to consider anticipation. With a running jump, there will be no possibility of a more conventional "opposite direction" anticipation occurring. This is because to have the character move in the opposite direction to the jump, we would have to have that character move backward before moving forward again—entirely breaking the rhythm and momentum of the lead-up run. So, the way an Olympic jumper prepares for a long jump is to sink the hips down just before the take-off.

On the assumption that our character is going to jump from her left leg, we will tend to put a bend in the leg that she is going to jump from while she is still running—in this case, the left leg. To give a reason for the jump, I have added a number of rocks in the way of the running character, so she has to jump over them to avoid them.

Note the deeper bend on the left leg as the character is about to jump, compared to the normal bend in the leg during the running action.

To emphasize this idea a little more, I have added a slight slow-in/slow-out around the maximum bend position.

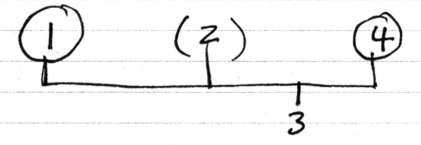

From the leg bend down (which is the effective anticipation of the jump up), the character must drive up to the apex position on the jumping arc and then bring her legs forward to effect a safe landing.

143

Again, seeing this jumping action as being similar to a bouncing ball, we must add a slow-in and slow-out to the top of the action arc, too, giving us a greater sense of the gravity affecting the action. The slow-in to the top will suggest gravity pulling the jumper downward, whereas the slow-out from the top will suggest the force of gravity accelerating the character downward from that apex position. Here is what the charts will look like to demonstrate this idea.

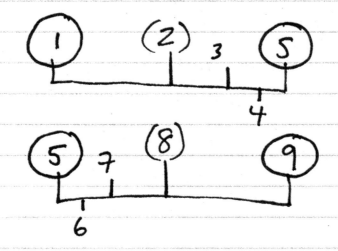

And here is what the actual frames of the action looked like when everything was complete.

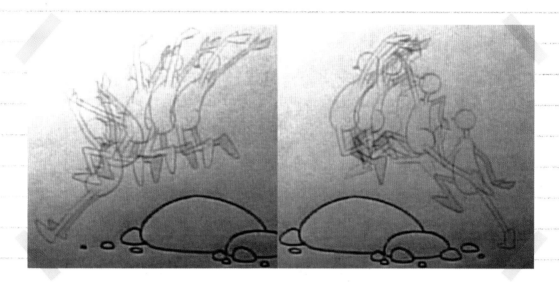

Note especially that with the "hit" landing key position, the legs need to be in **advance** of the body when the heels actually touch the ground. The legs in this case will tend to act as a break on the forward velocity of the running/jumping character. Without the legs thrown forward to break this forward momentum, the character would simply rotate forward out of control and fall flat on her face on the ground in front of her.

Now having landed, the character will need to be seen doing the breaking of that forward momentum, so she can rise to a standing, upright position at the end of the jump. This means that we have to put in a squash/cushion position after the hit so that the character can move downward before finally standing upright.

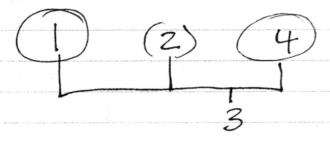

Again, a judicious use of a slow-in toward the end of the squash position will make this action that much more convincing. This is what the action will look like when all the in-between positions are added.

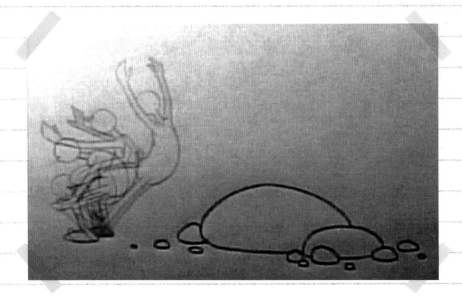

Finally, we have to bring the character up to a straight and standing position from the previous squash position.

Again, our friend the slow-in will make this all the more convincing. Here's the chart we will use to effect this move.

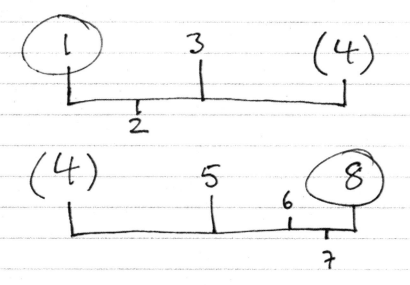

And here are the frames that reflect this charted action.

If completed successfully and accurately, the entire running jump will look like the example on the website.

Of course, there will be many ways of doing an alternative approach to the running jump, but this generic version will give you a strong foundation on which to build your own approach. Remember that to get distance along the ground with your jump, you will have to increase the speed of the character's run while keeping the jumping height and arc flatter. On the other hand, if you want height rather than distance on your jump, you will tend to keep the approach run slower, the squash down lower, and the height of the actual jump more elevated. In real life this will tend to reduce the distance covered on the ground somewhat, too.

As with all animation, you are strongly urged to research the kind of jump you want to do before you even consider animating it. The standard process of approaching animation is first to create thumbnail key pose sketches based on real life observation. If you cannot observe the action going on in real life, seek out film footage that matches the kind of action you are trying to create. If that footage is not available, shoot it for yourself on a video camera. Ultimately, with such footage available to you, you will be better able to observe and analyze what is going on with the action and how you might better create more dynamic keys that represent it.

Remember too that you should not simply copy your live-action reference material—you should caricature and exaggerate it to get the maximum effect in animation. This is what your thumbnail, key-frame sketches are all about. They will allow you to first analyze the dynamic action of all the key positions but then will enable you to extend and exaggerate them to the point where you can use them to create more dynamic and convincing action.

Suggested Assignment

Find a real-life jumping action that appeals to you. It might be an Olympic long jumper, a gymnast, a circus acrobat, or just a kid jumping from her bed to the ground. But sketch and/or film the action to understand exactly what is going on in real time and real motion. Then attempt to replicate it, first through key thumbnail sketches and then through more complete, exaggerated poses. Shoot this as a pose test first, without in-betweens but timed out to match your first inclinations. Adjust the timings as you see fit.

Next, block in your in-betweens. But remember that, like the bouncing ball action, all jumping action will take place on arcs and therefore you will not be strictly in-betweening your main action but finding in-between positions that have to be relocated along the path of that arc. Shoot and/or render your action in real time, to ascertain how it is working. Polish and adjust further until you achieve that movement that perfectly replicates the original reference footage but caricatured to work better in the animated medium.

chapter 8

Weight

The creation of weight in animation is something that challenges many animators. Far too many characters and objects that are poorly animated tend to float around as if they are of no volume or mass at all—or more importantly, they are impervious to the effects of gravity. However, the animation that really works, that convinces us that the characters are working and existing within a real world subject to the laws of that real world, are those that have an element of weight integrated into their movement.

Weight is not an easy quality to define, but there are essential core rules and principles that we can add to our animation that make everything we do more convincing. In the previous notebook on jumps, we began to hint at weight from the perspective of a bouncing ball. Let's delve into this concept a little more now and explore the qualities of weight and its approaches, using the bouncing ball illustration.

First let's remind ourselves of what the animated frames of a standard bouncing rubber ball will look like.

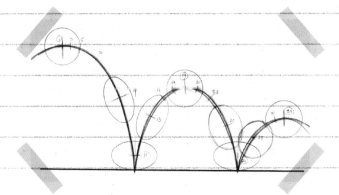

Now go to the website to see what it looks like in motion.

Now let's explore what happens with a lighter object and a heavier object. For the lighter object we will consider a falling leaf; for the heavier one we will consider a dropping cannonball. Clearly this comparison will give us an idea of weight in action.

Falling Leaf

The thing to remember about a falling leaf in terms of weight is that it contains very little mass or weight. It is also uniquely responsive when it comes to the forces of gravity air resistance. This means that its falling action will not be direct or even predictable compared to a heavier object like a cannonball. Consequently, the way it moves from top to bottom will be subtle and meandering.

Additionally, because a leaf has aerodynamic surfaces it will tend to be more responsive to air resistance than another object; therefore, it will tend to soar and glide in its motion, rather than drop down more mechanically like a regular ball. Consequently its movement will be more poetic and unevenly timed, like the previous sequence I animated for my BAFTA award-winning film *Hokusai: An Animated Sketchbook*.

Cannonball

By contrast, the quality of a cannonball is entirely different. A cannonball is clearly far heavier than most other balls, indicating that it will have less bounce to its hard and unresponsive mass.

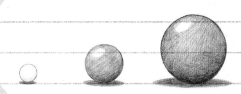

Not being either resilient or particularly dynamic in itself, the cannonball will move very little and slowly. For example, unlike the falling leaf, a cannonball will not rise at all fast if thrown into the air—such is its weight—and therefore such will be the extreme forces of gravity working on it. This will be different if it is fired upward by a cannon, of course, but even then the weight of the cannonball will bring it down to earth much faster than either a rubber ball or a ping-pong ball.

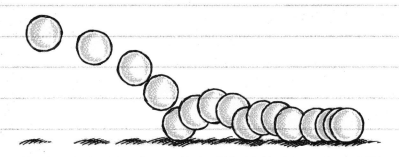

Also, having a solid and unyielding mass, the cannonball will not bounce high when it hits the ground, if at all on a very soft surface. Instead, if the surface is especially soft, like grass, it is more likely that the cannonball will become embedded in the grass at the first point of landing, or if it bounces at all it will leave a huge impact mark on the ground, with perhaps another, less dramatic indentation at the site of where it next bounces to!

The Lesson

The lesson in all this is that one way of indicating weight with your animation is to consider the impact the moving mass makes on the environment around it, or else the degree to which gravity or air resistance will impact its movement.

Indicate **weight** by the impact the moving mass has on its environment, or the degree to which gravity or air resistance impacts its movement.

In the old Disney internship training system (which sadly no longer exists), students were required to create a "flour sack" animated sequence. The flour sack was literally a floppy-looking canvas sack filled with baking flour; the student was required to animate the sack, giving it a quality of weight, flexibility, and mass. Consequently, the original design of the flour sack and the way it was drawn have to suggest this before it is even animated!

Disney students were encouraged to animate the sack, doing some kind of action within a predescribed scene that emphasized the weight, mass, and flexibility of the flour sack. Essentially, the action was pretty similar to a bouncing ball in many ways, but the additional factors of the sack's floppiness and its deformation when it hits hard surfaces has to be defined in action, too.

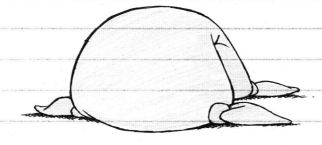

The flour sack exercise is an excellent one for all student and novice animators to attempt because the quality of weight and bounce are at the forefront of its success and believability.

The Pose Is Everything!

This is a phrase I will use over and over again when it comes to animation, especially character animation, and it is no less true when it comes to defining weight in animated movement. It is certainly true of the flour sack assignment mentioned earlier, and it will therefore be no less true when it comes to full character animation.

In terms of animation with weight, it implies that it is the key poses you create for your character that will determine how weighty your action will look. For example, here is a character carrying a heavy box.

However, this pose suggests that the box is not at all heavy and therefore nothing subsequently done with the animation will convince us that it indeed is heavy. On the other hand, the following pose definitely communicates to its audience that the same box is suddenly much heavier.

This one looks a little less heavy,

whereas this one does suggest weight.

What is it about the more successful poses that make the box look heavy compared to the ones that don't? Well, first and foremost it is the adjustment of the bodily posture that immediately communicates to the viewer that the box is heavy and therefore the body is somewhat struggling to deal with it. For example, looking at one of the previous drawings again, see how the character is leaning backward to accommodate the extra balance that is required to counteract the additional weight that is in front of it.

Note that in a previous chapter we talked about balance, instructing that unless a character is meant to be falling over, all the weight of that character has to be balanced evenly over its point of contact on the ground. Consequently, with a heavy box being held in front of the character, it will automatically have to adjust its pose accordingly, so both the weight of its body and the weight of the box are balanced evenly over its feet on the ground.

Note also that in this pose the legs are bent to accommodate the extra weight that is being carried. When we are standing normally, there should be a slight bend to the knees—not too much but just a little to help us adjust and maintain our normal balance. However, the more additional weight that is carried, the more the legs will tend to bend, unless the weight is too heavy, of course, and the legs will collapse beneath us!

Note finally that the head is pulled backward and the face is straining upward. These are all additional clues to the audience that the box being carried is very heavy.

Remember to do this in all the other poses you might put your character through if he is dealing with extremes of weight—or even if he himself is a heavy character attempting to move.

If a character is bending down to pick up a heavy weight, make sure that the poses you choose will reflect the sense of weight required to make it convincing. For example, if the weight is really heavy, there is no point in having the weight set away from the feet in front of the character. Instead, the character will somehow have to get both feet as close to the weight as possible—either side, if absolutely possible—and not just lift the weight with the arms but with the legs and the back, too.

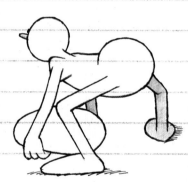

Let's also remember the basic warnings we get from medical advisors when we attempt to pick up heavy weights to avoid putting out a vertebra or two. We need to keep our backs straight and remain as upright as possible when the weight rises. We are additionally told to use our legs as much as possible to initiate the upward momentum, since the legs are far stronger than the arms or the back.

Remember that with heavy weights, the arms are merely the supporting, containing, and guiding elements in the exercise anyway, with the legs making the bulk of the effort. This is because the arms are by far weaker than the legs, and therefore it is to the legs we must look for getting the bulk of the weight moving.

For a clearer explanation of this concept, check out film footage of a weightlifter doing a "clean and jerk" action.

Weight in Movement

Characters dealing with weight in movement also have to be specially adapted in the way they move. For example, a heavy character walking will not walk the same way as a thin person walking. A very heavy person will have a greater side-to-side action on each stride because he has to adjust far more the distribution of weight over the contact position to get balance over the contact foot.

Similarly, when reaching a passing position on his walk, a heavy character will more than likely angle his free leg knee outward more so that he can maneuver his thickened thighs around each other.

Then, when a heavy person brings his free leg down to the hit position on a stride, a slight bend in the knee of the front leg tends to follow—at least until it reaches the next passing position, by which time the contact leg beneath the character should be pretty much straight again.

Obviously, the more weight the character is carrying, the greater the bend in the lead leg after the front leg hit.

Other factors that might be considered with a large person moving are the overlapping actions that will be witnessed in the stomach region. Remember, with so much fat in front, the whole soft tissue in the front stomach area will be much more fluid than the rest of the body. Consequently, when the body mass is moving down in an action, the soft and more flexible stomach mass will tend to stay up a little longer. Similarly, when the body mass is moving upward, the stomach mass will tend to hold down a little longer behind it.

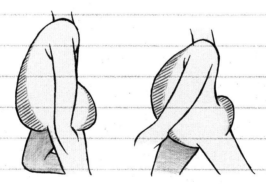

Moving Weight

More likely, most animation will involve the moving of a prop in addition to just body movement. This also has to communicate a sense of weight in the prop. Of course, if the character is moving a feather, there will be absolutely no adjustment to the action, since there is no significant weight or mass involved at all. However, if the character is trying to move a heavy weight around, there will be significant adjustment to the bodily action.

Anticipation

We will deal more fully with anticipation in another chapter. For now I will just say that in order to move a heavy weight, some degree of anticipation will be involved.

Essentially, the rules of anticipation state that to more effectively move something in one particular direction, it helps to first move it a little in the opposite direction, to make a more dynamic main action.

To illustrate weight and anticipation in action, let's consider a character throwing a flour sack from one place to another. If we animate the character simply standing upright, holding the sack in her arms and immediately throwing it in the direction required, it will not demonstrate to the audience that there is much manipulation of weight going on.

However, if we adjust the initial pose a little—even bending the character's legs a bit—it already tells the audience that the object being held is heavy, even before it is thrown. Then, if we have the character swing the sack a little in a backward direction first to give a greater momentum for the ultimate throw forward, it will be far more convincing for that audience to believe that a heavy sack is being negotiated and not a light one.

Similarly, if a character is wielding a huge and heavy sword and swiping an unknown enemy with it, it will not be convincing to the audience if there is no adjustment to the body posture, even just to hold the sword.

For example, there is no adjustment to the body here so the sword looks like it has no weight whatsoever!

Consequently, you should adjust the character's posture to suggest it has adjusted to the weight of the sword.

Then, when swiping with the sword around, make sure that there is a little anticipation to start the action.

Similarly, when the swipe is made, make it on a wide arching path of action, with the body leaning a little backward to accommodate the extreme weight and velocity acting on the body.

Finally, at the end of the swipe, do not simply stop the action dead, since doing so will again imply that the sword does not have weight. Instead, extend the sword's action far further than the ultimate final position, giving it a sense of greater weight by employing this extreme overlapping action.

To make this even more effective, add a slow-in to the final action from the end of the swipe to the end of the overlapping extreme position. This will give it a much more convincing sense that the sword is heavy and proving hard to stop.

A slow-in action from the extreme position back to the final static position will only increase the illusion of weight. Even then, if the sword is being held out but the character has stopped moving overall, you might want to add a slow dip to the end of the sword as time goes by, to suggest that the weight of the sword is increasing, weakening the wrist of the character.

And don't forget that to move weight from a static position you will need to suggest extra effort at the beginning to get it going. Therefore, adding a slow-out from the initial static position will give an added sense of effort; that is, the action needs to start slowly and then accelerate as more momentum is achieved.

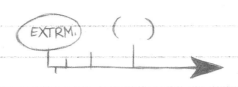

In Conclusion

All these tips will suggest ways that you can add weight to your action. I'm sure they can be applied in a million different ways to a million different actions. However, if you get the principle of it set in your mind, you will find that your animation has more weight to it when, or if, this is desired. Always seek out other ways of adding weight to your action. Action with weight—as opposed to animation without weight—is what effectively separates the pros from the novices.

Here are a few reminders of things I also mentioned in my book, *How to Make Animated Films* (Focal Press) that will help you communicate greater weight in your character animation.

1. In posing a character that is dealing with weight, remember that the strongest parts of the human body are the legs, and therefore they need to bend to cushion the impact any weight places on them.

2. Where there is an absence of weight, however, or even the opposite of weight (such as when a character has a helium balloon strapped to his back), the poses can imply the opposite.

3. The heavier a thing is, the slower it moves or can be moved. Therefore, if your character is carrying a great deal of weight or is very heavily built itself, be prepared to slow the action to communicate this fact.

4. Lifting a weight from the ground will initially be difficult for a character to do. Therefore, employ some preparatory action to communicate that the character is finding it hard to achieve, use a "slowing-out" chart timing for the initial raising of the weight so that it slowly accelerates upward until the character can gain leg thrust to achieve the added momentum required for the lift.

5. If a character is built heavily or at least has a certain amount of weight around his or her stomach, butt, or breasts, remember to employ some overlapping action on these areas to indicate that there is indeed weight there responding to ups and downs and changing velocity of the overall body.

6. Because of gravity, weight always tends to drop downward. Consequently, characters carrying weight or characters with weight in their physical make-up may often suggest a downward sag to their pose or in the flesh of their body.

7. In seeking to lift a heavy weight, a character has a much stronger base to work from if she separates her feet and applies the lift over a greater area for the pulling-up action.

8. When a character walks carrying a weight or is very heavily built, his balance and movement will be significantly modified. Also, a character carrying a substantially heavy weight cannot possibly take as large strides as a character not carrying anything.

9. A very fat person will not be able to walk the same way a thin person can, since she has to overcompensate for her side-to-side lean on each step—that is, to adjust her balance, which will enable her better to move her free leg around the contact leg due to the excessively fat, heavy nature of her thighs.

10. In order for a character to move a very heavy weight that he is carrying, he will first have to use a certain amount of anticipation (or swing in the opposite direction) to get some kind of momentum going.

Suggested Assignment

Study a weightlifter in action. Thumbnail a few sketchbook pages of keyframe poses that give you a caricatured sense of the action that is taking place.

For this assignment, if you can view the weightlifter's action from more than one viewpoint, it will be much the better for your understanding of what is going on.

Ideally, you should go to a weightlifting event and sketch or film what is going on. Then analyze the timing and the way that slow-ins and slow-outs can be used to suggest the struggle of moving a very heavy weight against the force of gravity.

Finally, animate the action based on all your research, and adjust as necessary. The ultimate exercise is for the audience to really believe that your character is moving a heavy weight; you will succeed with this exercise only if that occurs.

Arcs and Anticipation

Arcs

Have you ever watched leaves falling from the trees? Have you noticed that they don't drop straight down but tend float on ever-diminishing arcs, much like the animation I did for my film, *Hokusai: An Animated Sketchbook***?**

An arc is the core of all movement. As I have said before, only a very fixed mechanical device moves in straight lines; everything else moves in curves or arcs in accordance with their mass or weight. Of course, if the leaves on a tree were round and made of solid iron, they would drop straight down like a stone, or apples. But they are not. They are made of thin, light, aerodynamic surfaces that tend to cause them to glide downward in arced seesaw swings or curved, spiraling nosedives.

This is, of course, an extreme example of arcs in action, but it is a good one that illustrates the fact that all things tend to move in some form of arc. In nature, for instance, it is said that movement in arcs is the most natural action possible. In animation too, arcs create a more rhythmic, flowing movement, giving your animation great strength and dynamism.

A lack of the use of arcs has mainly been the product of laziness on the part of the animator. In traditional 2D animation, assistant animators find that it is much harder to interpret the in-betweens on a curved path of action rather than in a straight line, as conventional in-betweens would suggest. Similarly, lazy 3D animators prefer to let the computer software decide the direction and placement of the in-betweens—which will be automatically straight and predictable—rather than go in and adjust each one of the in-between positions to enable the action to move more on the curve of an arc.

However, if animation is to be really good and really convincing, the animator must accept the inevitability of arcs.

Let's state the obvious and return to the bouncing ball illustrations I used in the earlier chapter. When a standard rubber ball bounces, it not only bounces successively lower and shorter as the action unfolds, but all those bounces will follow a path of action that is consistently arced.

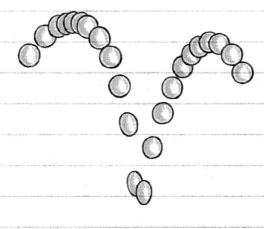

This arced action doesn't apply only to bouncing balls. If you fire an iron ball from a cannon or kick a soccer ball down a pitch, it will always follow an arced path of action because at first it flies freely, but slowly the forces of gravity slow it and drag it back earthward again. Even in long distance air travel, pilots fly planes on extended arcs from the start to end destinations to make the journey shorter.

For a commercial, I once animated a character that fell and bounced and dropped to its eventual headlong crash into a snow bank. It was because of the arcs I used that the action worked so well.

I also animated a character falling down an animation desk for my parody of a Pinocchio sequence in *Endangered Species*. Again, the use of arcs made the action look believable.

But arcs do not apply only to bouncing balls, falling leaves, or planes in the sky. The use of arcs can be very subtle and unexpected. For example, if you put a simple generic walk together and look at the arced patterns of the action, you will begin to notice just how subtle and all-pervading is the presence of arcs in all movement. This is how the work looks for two strides—note the arced flow of the head as it moves up and down.

Now here is the walk where the arcs on the head, shoulders, wrists, hips, and ankles are marked. Look at the changing flowing patterns that these arching points make.

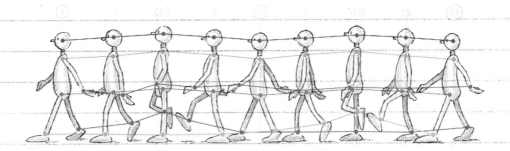

For comparison, here is a generic run cycle.

And here are all the same arc plot points for this action.

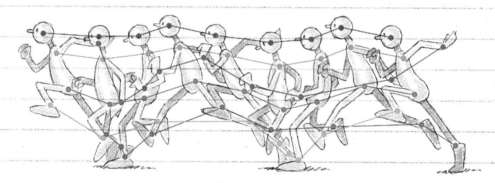

Next, let's look at the same effect with a character pitching a ball.

See how the arc paths are so much more diverse, meaning that the more dynamic the action, the more the use of arcs will come into play.

However, even with a simple action, the mature animator should think of how to integrate arcs into the movement at all times. For example, if a character's hand is putting a glass down onto a surface, the logical thing to do is make it a direct action.

But if you really want to make your animation smooth and natural looking, you might consider alternatives. For example, you might want to move the glass on a downward arc as it moves forward, with the bottom of the glass dragging behind.

You then might take the glass just beyond and above the end position and bring it down on a slightly less downward arc, with the bottom of the glass again delaying.

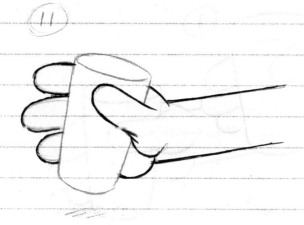

By adding a slow-in/slow-out at the extreme end of both arc actions, you might give a better sense of timing to the entire thing.

Similarly, consider a character pushing a doorbell button. The conventional thing to do would be to have the hand in-between straight to the button for the push.

However, if you use an upward arc to a point just above the push position, then use another subtle arc down to the push, it will make the entire thing more attractive and fluid.

There are a million ways that arcs can be added to animated movement. I've spoken previously and often about the generic head turn. Quite often animators will just in-between a head position from one direction to another.

However, the correct way to do that would be to have a dropped breakdown position (sometimes an elevated breakdown position would work, too) and then in-between the head to follow a downward (upward) arc that matches this.

This approach gives a much more natural movement to the head's action.

Similarly with the eyes: If a character is looking in one direction and you want to have him adjust his look to another direction, the traditional suggestion is that you put a blink in the middle of the action so that it appears more dynamic.

However, if you have the eyeball hint at a downward arced path beneath the eyelid as it does so, it will feel even more natural.

Finally, let's go to the website to look at very brief piece of animation that, like the scene of leaves falling at the top of the tutorial, I created for my *Hokusai ~ An Animated Sketchbook* film.

The action appears very quick and simple on screen, but it was nevertheless necessary for me to show the character's versatility and expertise in the film. Therefore, although it is very quick in screen time—barely a second for the action to happen—I wanted it to be smooth and effective. Essentially it shows the character moving from one position to another, and it would have been very easy for me to have animated mechanically from one to the other. However, I wanted it to be a little more flowing and rhythmic than that, so I in-betweened the action on arcs in the main areas, giving it a more fluid sense of action. Here are the arc traces in question (red for the head, green for the left wrist, and blue for the right wrist).

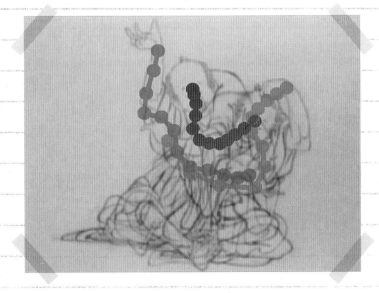

Remember, when you use arcs, you are refining the action. You are giving it more fluidity and rhythm. But do not use arcs for the sake of using arcs, since sometimes a straightforward mechanical approach with the movement from A to B is best done with no deviation in the path of action at all.

However, also never forget that most of nature does not move in straight lines, so you are well advised to consider the judicious use of arcs with most of your action. Never overuse arcs if you can help it, for sometimes extremes of curved action can be distracting from the core motion you are trying to communicate to the audience. But where there are broad, sweeping movements—such as a dancer in action, a conductor guiding an orchestra, or a golfer driving off from a tee—the use of broad, curved, arced movements is essential.

Anticipation

I always begin my lecture on anticipation with reference to Newton's third law, which suggests that for every action there is an equal and opposite reaction. This statement holds the key to what anticipations are all about.

Indeed, I often suggest that we might hijack this truism to suggest that animation's first law should be, "For each and every action there is a subtle and opposite anticipation!"

Anticipation

For every action, there is a subtle and opposite anticipation!

Even the ancient tradition of Tai Chi reflects this understanding by indicating that before any major movement in one direction, a practitioner makes a slight and subtle movement in the opposite direction first. This in essence is what anticipation really is.

We might boil the concept down to the simple statement that in order for dynamic movements to be more powerful and communicative, they should first have a little reverse movement in the opposite direction before moving in the intended direction. For example, a character is about to stand up from a sitting position. To get more impetus it helps if she first leans backward before moving forward and upward. This is a perfect opportunity to use anticipation to aid the action.

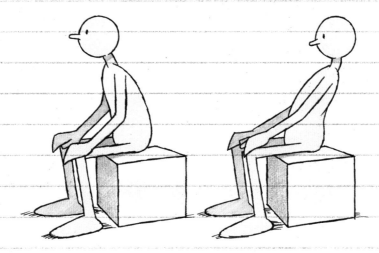

Let's also use the example from the weight chapter—a character tossing a heavy flour sack. If that character simply threw the flour sack from a standing position, it wouldn't go very far nor would it look particularly heavy! However, if there were first a backswing to preempt the toss, the sack would suggest weight and it would be far easier to convince the audience that it could travel a long way.

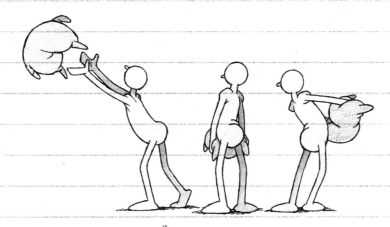

Anticipation does not simply apply to the swinging of weights, however. Every single animated action, from the simple turning of a head to the beginning of a jump and even to the lifting of a pen from a desk, can benefit from the use of anticipation.

Watch a housecat pounce. It won't simply jump. Instead it will first sink back a little onto its haunches, wiggle its butt, and then, with a short but even more extreme squat on its hind legs, jump forward with a great sense of power and dynamism

I think we are all aware of the early Warner Brothers cartoons where characters run off fast. Initially they will wind up slowly in the opposing direction, slowing into the end position; then they will scrabble forward dramatically in an almost total blur. Sometimes they will not even be seen running—they will simply execute a finely tuned anticipatory wind-up in the opposite direction and then invisibly be gone, leaving an unfolding cloud of dust in their wake.

I've mentioned the following idea in some of my previous writings, but I will refer to it again to make the point. Watch a cowboy go for his gun in a holster. He will first slightly lift his hand up and open his fingers a little and then thrust his hand down to grab and draw the gun from his holster. To increase the effect, he might make the whole thing more effective by first pushing the gun down a little in the holster before pulling it out forward, ready to fire.

Every single animated action, if it is to be a significant action, will need to have some form of effective anticipation employed at the beginning to make it more impactful and dramatic. For example, let's again examine a character that throws a punch.

Perhaps this move can look reasonably effective if we simply in-between it from pose to pose. However, if the punching hand is animated backward a short way first, as an anticipation to the main movement, the thrown punch and its impact will be that much more effective. Put the punch on a slight outward arc and that punch could look even more rock solid and convincing!

To emphasize the point, let's look at the example of a baseball pitcher as he pitches a ball. I often show the example of a badly animated throwing action first by way of comparison.

Note how flat and unconvincing it looks. There is no power or sense of dynamic to the action.

Now let's look at some much more dynamic key poses, with an anticipation added. See how the whole thing already looks more dynamic and natural looking.

FYI: Here are the charts that I planned for those keys.

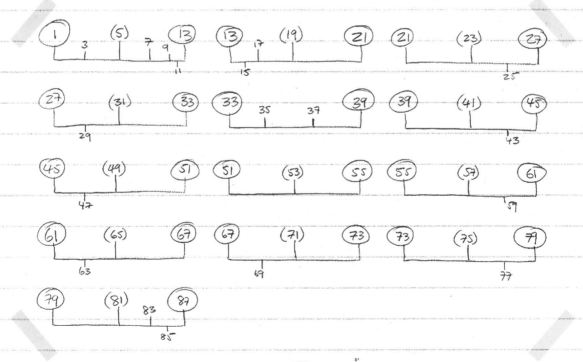

Now, pulling the whole thing together, on the website you can see the final action. Note the way the anticipation sets up the major action. Without it, the action would look much flatter and unconvincing.

I guess I should indicate that the breakdown drawings for the key positions in this movement are somewhat eccentric. Here's what some of them look like.

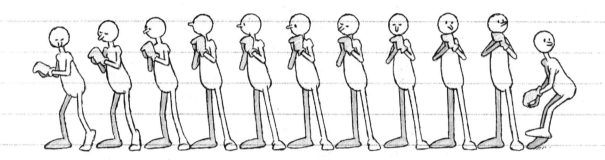

Note that often it is necessary to not have the breakdown positions at the logical midway points, as the preceding indicates. Like use arcs and the amounts that the arcs are exaggerated, adjusting midpoint breakdown poses is a process that comes from experience. However, an intensive study of any reference footage you might have at your disposal will certainly give you strong cues as to how you approach any breakdown you create.

A hint at what I'm talking about here can be seen in how the body leads the action throughout the pitch, yet the actual pitching arm whips through at the very last moment, giving a final dynamic kick to the action. Even minor anticipations are important!

Anticipations should always be considered, even for the smallest of movements. If eyes are to look in one particular direction, it helps a lot if you take them a little in the opposite direction first, maybe even with a blink added to the anticipation or even at the midpoint of the transition from one direction to another.

I have learned that blinking the eyes on an anticipation will definitely give a greater impact to the look when the eyes are finally open.

Next, let's go back again to the character that stands up from a sitting position. The logical (and somewhat uninformed) way to handle this task will be to in-between the action mechanically, like so.

181

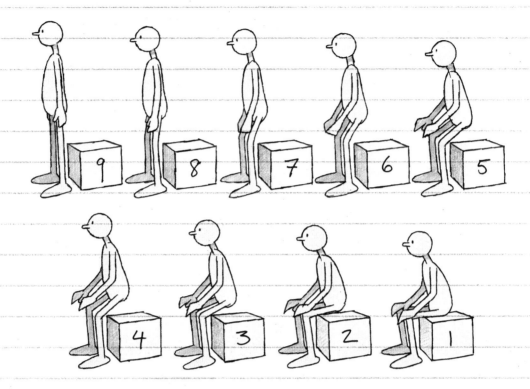

However, to make it more realistic and natural, it would help to have the character rock back a little before he stands, sliding their body mass over the legs before standing up.

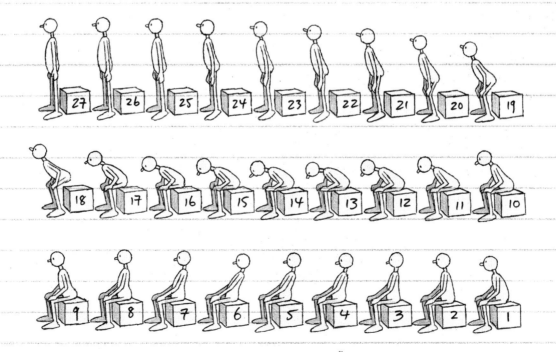

This way we will get a sense that the character is making an effort to get up and he is not just unnaturally rising from a static position. It will also give a sense of motivation for his body to rise. Go to the website for another example of a simple shock action where arcs are effective. Notice the effective use of the arced action on the head movement at the very end.

Anticipation can work really well in perspective, too. I have used this illustration before, but it does well to use it again here because it perfectly underlines the principles of anticipation.

A character is throwing a punch toward the camera lens. From a static position his fist fills the screen at the very end. It stops when it almost hits the screen.

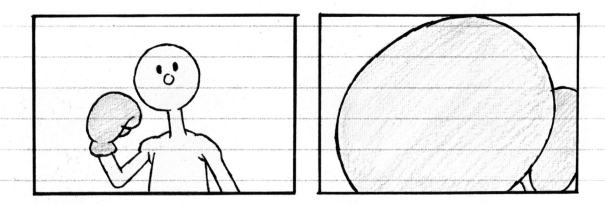

However, this action will work all the better if you anticipate it—that is, by first taking the fist farther away from the camera before it moves forward. This will give the entire thing far more depth and far more impact as the fist comes forward.

Indeed, if you actually bring the fist first farther forward than you ultimately want it to be at the end and then do a quick slow-in back to where you eventually want it, this will give an even greater sense of the hit to the audience—a kind of anticipation in reverse.

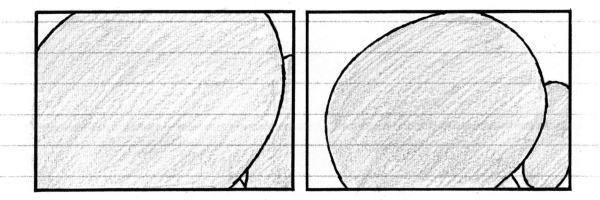

Anticipation can have all kinds of applications. For example, you can use one if a hand is pointing in a particular direction. Before you move it up and point in that direction, bring the hand back and down a little before you move it. A swipe with a sword or staff will look so much better if that sword or staff is drawn back first before swiping forward. If a character throws her head back to laugh out loud, first have her head and shoulders come down a little into her chest to anticipate it. If you are hitting a sound sync point for the laugh, this will make the actual hit on the sound of the laugh all the more powerful.

There is in fact no end to the varied and innovative ways you can apply anticipation or an action on an arc. In fact, the only way you can go wrong is not to use one in the first place!

Suggested Assignment

With a character of your own design, have that character putt a ball into a hole using a putting iron. Start the player in a static position, and then draw the club back in anticipation before making the putt. Seeing the ball drop into the hole, have the character jump up and down, swinging his club with delight. In addition to the anticipation on the club's backswing, find a way of having the delighted character move on arcs to emphasize his joy.

Overlapping Action

The core message of overlapping action is that not everything in an action—especially a character action—will move (or stop) at the same time. The biggest neglect of most inexperienced animators in either 2D or 3D animation is to put all the action of a character on the same keyframes. This is a major error.

To decide what is moving or what is the primary action and what is the secondary is something you have to quickly establish in your own mind. The primary action will dictate how the secondary action (or actions) goes. For example, a character with a cloak is running along with the cloak dragging behind him.

The character then suddenly stops, but the cloak, of course, does not. The same will occur if the character has long hair. The primary action (the figure running) may stop, but the secondary action (the cloak or the hair or whatever) will continue to move until it, too, comes to a halt later.

This concept is called overlapping action. It is also known as follow-through animation. We can split hairs about the difference between these two terms, but essentially they are all about the different speeds and timings that affect secondary animation in relation to primary action.

Overlapping action refers to the interplay of primary and secondary action. It is also known as follow-through animation.

Overlapping action needs to be applied to all animation where a character or object being animated has additional elements of varying weight and flexibility connected to it. For example, a flag being waved has two actions affecting it. The primary action is the staff of the flag that is being waved. The secondary action is the flag's material being tugged and following through on the staff.

Similarly, a package that is tossed with a ribbon loose on it will land pretty instantaneously, but the ribbon will drag behind, overlap the package's stopping position, and then finally come to a fluid halt beyond the package. This is also overlapping action.

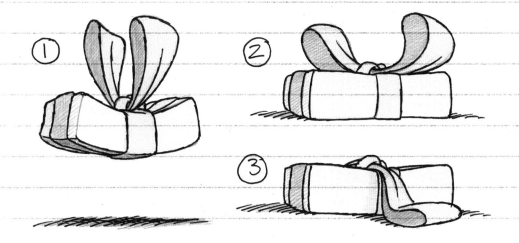

Even a mechanical-style character, like Wall-e, will have overlapping action. Indeed, that is what makes him look believable when he moves. For example, if a similar robot suddenly brings its body to a halt, its head and eye sections will continue moving, nodding decreasingly until they, too, come to a rest.

Overlapping Action on Hands

We discussed this in an earlier chapter, but we should reiterate the importance of overlapping action on a character's hands, especially with a walk.

With a walk it is really important to bring some fluidity and naturalness to the action; part of this process occurs by using the flexibility of the wrists to loosen up the entire arm action. We do this by adding drag to the hands. This means that, as indicated earlier in this book, when an arm moves forward on a stride, it is advised that you hold the hand back a little.

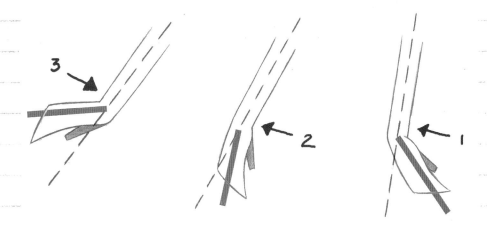

Then when the arm moves backward, hold the hand back in the opposite direction.

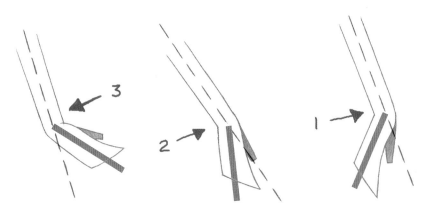

This will give a natural overlapping action to the arm that helps make the whole action look more natural.

Remember

When in-betweening a concave shape to a convex one, it works much better if you favor one side of the in-between position rather than a straight one. Here's what I mean in relation to the hand positions moving forward in a walk.

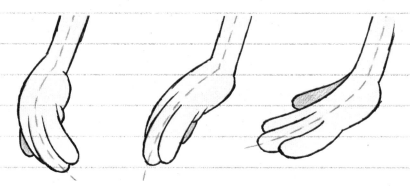

Here's a suggestion for when the arm is moving backward in the opposite direction.

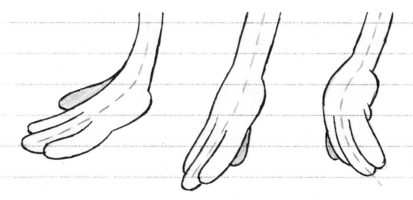

Hands actually give great opportunities for overlapping action in movements other than walks. For example, if a character presses a doorbell, it helps the action if the hand drags a little as the arm comes up and forward.

When it gets toward the end of the point action, it helps a little if the hand actually goes a little beyond the end position and then slows into the end position before the final point.

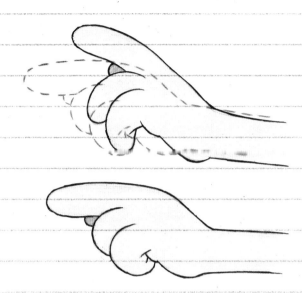

This is overlapping movement in action.

Similarly, you can use the neck when it comes to the head action. When the body is moving upward, hold the head down a little by tucking the chin in somewhat. Then, when the body is coming down the head should be held up a little, by having the chin stick out somewhat.

As we've discussed already, this principle can just as well be applied to quadruped action, where the shoulders, neck, and head can all be involved with the action.

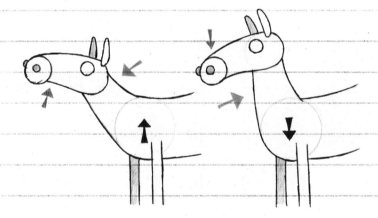

Overlapping action can be compared to the old Disney animator term, the successive breaking of joints. This also follows the principle that not everything moves at the same time and at the same speed. With successive breaking of joints there is a hierarchy of action. Picking up a pen from a desk does not begin with the fingers of the hand picking up the keys, but rather it starts with the body, then the shoulder, then the elbow, then the wrist, and finally the fingers. Even then the keys will probably show overlapping action as the hand comes to a halt.

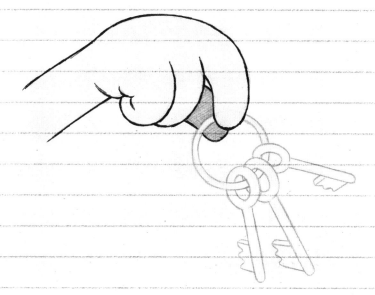

The keys bunched together on a key ring will be far more fluid than the hand and therefore will take longer to come to rest.

Overlapping action, or successive breaking of joints, is best described by a javelin thrower.

When we observe the sequence of a javelin throw, the action starts first at the hips, then the shoulders, elbows, wrists, and finally the hand.

Of course, such an explosive, dramatic action definitely needs a follow-through at the end. So, in the case of the javelin thrower, the head will move down and the throwing arm will wrap itself around the body after the throw.

If the throwing character has long hair, that too will overlap at the end of the throw and probably wrap itself over the eyes and face.

Hair

Hair offers the greatest opportunity for overlapping action in many cases.

See the website for an example of an action where the head turns one way to another.

However, if the head has hair, the hair will drag behind it like the animated example on the companion website.

This is overlapping action on the hair. The key to this movement is the fact that when the head stops moving, the hair will continue to move. It will probably move backward and forward until it settles down to a stop position—unless the head begins to move again.

Whenever you're making overlapping moves like this, remember to use the principles of slowing-in and slowing-out to the in-between positions. I tend to use slow-ins to the extremes of the overlapping positions, as this chart indicates. The number of slow-in in-betweens will vary from action to action, of course, but the basic principle of deceleration will apply in each case.

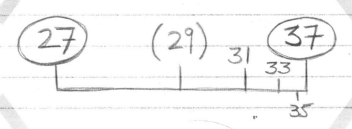

See the website for a sequence I used when I had dreadlocks moving on a separate level once the character's head stopped.

Random Use of Overlapping Action

Sometimes overlapping action can be really simple and not at all connected to natural movement. On the website, there is a quick scene I animated for my *Endangered Species* film that has a character looking up with his glasses on his forehead, only to have the glasses drop down onto his nose, to indicate a hint of surprise.

However, this little touch only required two key poses: glasses up …

…and glasses down!

Clothing

Another aspect of character animation that requires overlapping action is in clothing. Clothing is often fluid and secondary to the main body animation; therefore, it needs to be considered carefully if the action is to look convincing.

We have discussed the situation of a running caped character suddenly coming to a halt and the cape continuing to move until it too settles to a hold. This idea can apply to a tie, a scarf, a necklace—indeed, anything else that is free flowing and attached to the body.

For fast and economical animation against a deadline, overlapping action is probably something that has to take a back seat in an animator's priorities. But one look at the fabulous animation created at places like Disney and Pixar and you will see how much this adds to the reality and plausibility of animation.

I once recreated the action of the scene when Mickey Mouse walked down the steps in "The Sorcerer's Apprentice" sequence in the world's greatest animated masterpiece, *Fantasia*.

The character's cloak drags behind as the character walks, and it drops off each of the steps as he descends.

Note also the very slight overlapping on the hat, which has a slight back and forward motion on each of the character's steps.

The Nature of Cloth

It might pay us to give a little attention to the way we attempt to present the material make-up of clothing when we're animating overlapping action. This means that we have to consider whether the cloth is fluid or stiff, thick or thin, heavy or light.

Many years ago, at the beginning of my career at the Richard Williams studio in London, we all heard the late, great Disney master animator, Art Babbit, give a series of lectures on many things that the Disney animators had evolved over the years. One of them was the nature of cloth in overlapping action.

Art explained that even the way we draw cloth communicates certain things to the audience. For example, if the cloth is of a heavy nature, it is far better if the animator draws the corners of the cloth with a round and thick look, like so.

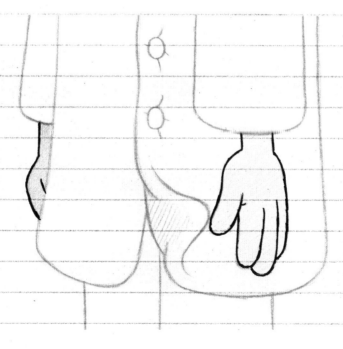

However, if the cloth is thin and light, it is much better to animate the cloth with sharp, square corners.

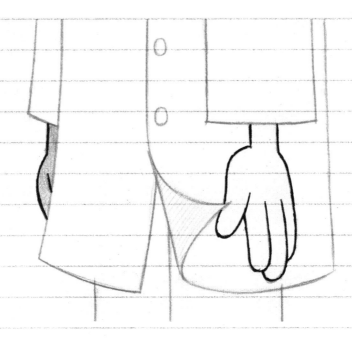

Art felt that this technique sets up the audience psychologically, before the movement even begins. Thick and heavy cloth does indeed look more rounded than thin and light cloth, and merely drawing it that way will communicate to the audience the quality of the material we are animating when we move it. Of course, the way we move it has to reflect the way it looks too!

Thick and heavy cloth will move more slowly and sluggishly, as we hinted in the earlier chapter that deals with weight. This too will affect the way the character moves, of course, since the character will be less free when wearing thick and heavy clothing as opposed to thin and light material. Using lots of slow-ins with sluggishly overlapping clothing will somewhat reflect this weight.

However, if the clothing is light and flimsy, the character will be able to move more freely and faster. Light clothing will also require a faster and more responsive overlapping action in the cloth too—hence the need for the animator to pay attention to these things.

Here are two characters that suggest the thick and heavy clothing that they were required to wear in a winter commercial I once directed and animated.

Notice too that we even animated the steam as they spoke, and yet another form of secondary/overlapping action after the primary action of the speaking mouth was established.

Keep Things Moving!

It is never good to entirely stop a character animating while it is on the screen. However, if you really need to stop the figure action for any reason, use of secondary movement through overlapping action can help keep everything alive on the screen when the major action stops. It's like a Warner Brothers-style character crashing into a wall and then bits of the character's body shattering into pieces and falling off while the bulk of the body is impacted on the wall!

I think animation purists will suggest that many of the examples I have used here can be called overlapping action, whereas others should be assigned to the term follow-through. However, I tend to consider the two terms as pretty much the same things. If we did want to split hairs, I would suggest that overlapping action occurs when the primary action stops and the secondary action continues after it. This will be defined by the flexibility, fluidity, lightness, and mass of the secondary material being animated.

Follow-through is associated more with the end result of an action, where the whole body of a character or object is arriving at a conclusion and yet parts of that body or object are continuing through as their peripheral velocity causes them to continue moving at a faster rate. I am thinking here of the arm on our javelin thrower, or the passengers in a car when it comes to an abrupt halt, or even the sword of a warrior at the end of a big swipe as we discussed earlier.

Bottom line: I think the edges blur when it comes to defining both actions in every case. Consequently, as long as you remember that not all aspects of a character or object are equal—and that some are more equal than others when it comes to their speed and the way they animate—it doesn't really matter what you call it, as long as you do it!

Of course, great animation has been created without any overlapping action at all. Some of the finest cartoon films ever created disobey all natural laws, and therefore overlapping or follow-through animation goes out the window. However, if you are trying to create the "plausible implausible world," that Walt Disney described, the use of overlapping action or follow-through action will be something you should not ignore.

Staggers

Not quite overlapping action, but there are times when you can be really creative when it comes to secondary action on a primary action. The following is not entirely using overlapping action or follow-through animation, but it is a way of thinking that will bring something extra to your animation.

At one time in my career I was asked to animate a character nervously walking along a diving board.

I first thought of having the character's knees knock and shake as he walked along the board, but I found a quicker and more effective way of doing it by employing a **stagger**.

Staggers are ways of using the notion of creative in-betweening to create an agitated or vibrating movement. Imagine an arrow hitting a target and you will know what I mean. A traditional animation way of doing this is to have two keys for the arrow sticking in the target—one with the end of the arrow sticking up and one with the arrow bending down. A third (and final) key would be the arrow sticking straight in the target.

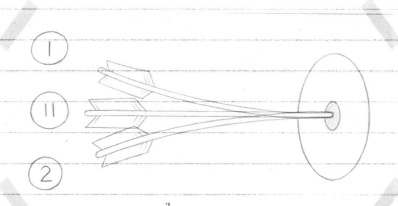

The process is quite easy. Create the in-betweens from the bent-up arrow to the perfectly straight arrow. These can be numbered as odd numbers. Here is a chart I would recommend.

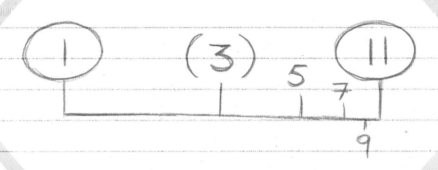

Next create the in-betweens of the bent-down arrow to the perfectly straight one and number these on even numbers.

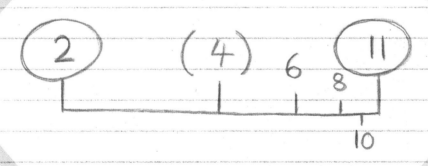

Finally, interleave the in-betweens in the correct numerical order and film them. When they are played back, the arrow will bounce from an extreme up position to an extreme down position, to the next highest-up arrow to the next lowest-down arrow—and so on until the final frame becomes the perfectly straight one.

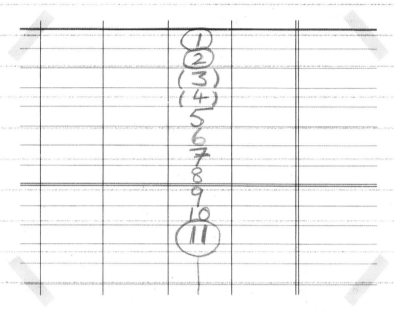

When this is played back on the screen, it will appear that the arrow hits the target with a violent vibration that rapidly reduces until it becomes perfectly still in the target.

I used this principle for the man on the diving board. I created all the odd numbers with the character walking along the board, with the diving board gradually turning up as he progresses.

Then I animated an identical walk sequence on even numbers, with the board progressively moving downward. (Note that the upper body is identical on both the odd and the even numbers.)

When the action was shot in numerical order, it gave the impression that the character was causing the board to vibrate up and down the farther he walked along it—further giving the impression that his legs were shaking more and more as he moved. A simple trick, but very effective!

Suggested Assignment

Do anything that will allow you to create secondary animation, or overlapping animation, with a character of your choice. However, if you want to recycle something you used before, why not put a flowing scarf around the neck of your character as it does a generic walk and run, and on a separate level have the scarf reacting to the character's body movement?

If you want an extra challenge, bring your character action to a halt and allow the scarf to move afterward until it eventually comes to a halt.

chapter 11

Fluidity and Flexibility

The biggest casualty in our age of changing computer technology designed to make the work of an animator quicker and easier is subtlety of approach, which is increasingly overlooked. Therefore, elements such as fluidity and flexibility in character animation need to be pursued more actively, even if they do take more time and effort, if animation is not to appear stiff or lackluster or have a certain wooden feel to it.

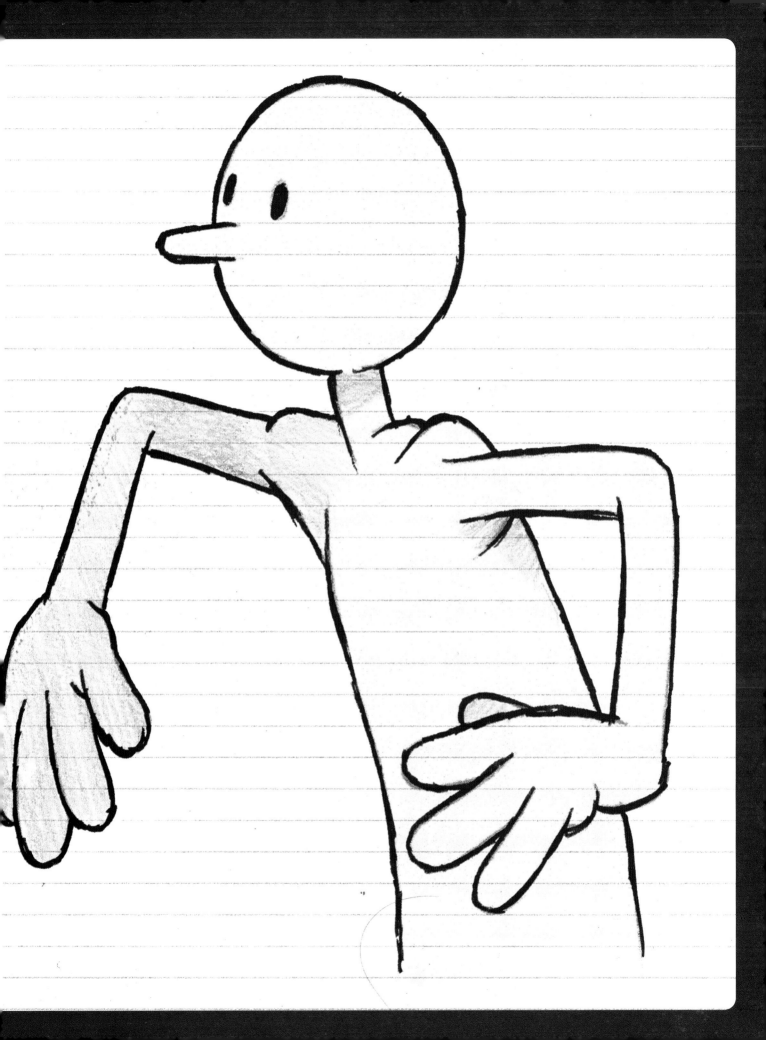

Flash animation in particular leads us into a world of an efficient, cut-out character animation style, but it does preclude things such as twist, rotation, and distortion in the case of full character animation—as exhibited in the best Disney or Pixar animated films.

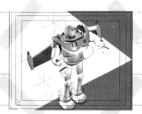

Shortcuts and economic advantage can be the benefits of digital age software, but for anyone who wants to pursue real character animation with natural depth, mass, and form, the advantages will never outweigh the disadvantages. Flexibility of movement can be achieved to some extent with technology-driven software, but fluidity is a greater challenge. That is why I still like to originate my animation on paper in the first instance—it gives me a tactile approach that enables a greater degree of sophistication in terms of movement.

So far the chapters in this book have armed everyone with enough process and principles of movement to tackle pretty much anything that is required of the animator. But what separates the average animator from the master animator is the subtlety of movement that defines characters and objects. Flexibility and fluidity of action are often missing from the everyday animator's approach.

We have to some extent already dealt with the principle of 'successive breaking of joints' earlier. However, it will not harm us to go back over this ground now, to help us understand that the flexibility that this technique achieves will work in pretty much every aspect of our animator's pallet of approaches.

Simply stated, the principle of successive breaking of joints means that with any major action there is a hierarchy of lesser actions that define that action. For example, if we consider the movement of a baseball pitcher, we will see this principle in action. The first thing we notice is that before the pitcher throws, there is a clear anticipation. In other words, before the ball is thrown forward, it is first pulled back.

Next we should consider the sequence of actions that makes up the throw. The primary action of these movements is the fact that the hip is brought forward first.

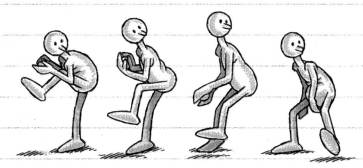

Next the shoulder comes through.

Then the elbow, and finally the wrist leading the hand.

Last but not least, there is the follow-through of the pitching arm that tends to wrap itself around the body after the effort of the throw.

This sequence of minor actions explains the full principle of successive breaking of joints, reminding us as animators that not everything moves at the same time, and therefore we should not animate it that way when it comes to establishing our key poses.

Go to the website to see what the pitcher looks like when he's animated.

Through this principle we can see that there is already a greater sense of flexibility to the action. This is how it should be for all actions we animate, large or small. Even a simple blink and head turn has its own sequence of events, and it pays us to research what happens in real life before we commit to any movement with our animation.

The really important thing to remember with regard to character animation is that the body is a fluid, flexible object and therefore it has to be treated as such when we move it. There are countless bones, joints, muscles, and fleshy tissue that need to be moved, often at different times and in different ways. However, the reality is that to move everything in a natural and fluid way, it can't all be contained on the same key poses with the same timings, as so much poor animation around today does. Consequently, knowledge of the anatomy and physical factors involved will assist us greatly in our pursuit of better animation.

Studying film or shooting specific reference footage is an excellent way for the animator to learn how components move in an action. Film yourself or someone else doing what you want the character to do, and you will learn a lot about physicality, timing, and weight distribution. You will learn ways of achieving fluidity and flexibility, too.

Indeed, if you are shooting footage as reference to your animation, I strongly recommend that you put tape markers on the body of the person being filmed, to give you a greater idea of the dynamics of movement involved. For example, a central tape down the center of the body and cross tapes on shoulders, hips, and chest will help you identify the various twists and turns the body goes through, even in the simplest of movements.

Student Megan Noble wisely using tape-referenced video to assist her animation.

I'm more and more convinced that with animation—specifically character animation—a rudimentary understanding of human (and animal) anatomy is a distinct advantage. I never thought this in my earlier years as an animator, but I am increasingly discovering that knowledge of how the human body basically works is a distinct advantage. With this kind of understanding it makes us better placed to utilize this knowledge when we're moving a character's inherent anatomy, especially when it comes to the movement of joints and the sequence of events that are called into play when these joints (and their accompanying muscles) are utilized.

When I talked about basic walks earlier I made the case for a simple twisting of the torso throughout the stride positions. When the right arm comes forward on a walk stride, the left leg will come forward, too, and vice versa for the next stride, and so on. This means that not only will the arms and legs come forward, but the shoulders and hips respectively will too. This additionally means that with the right shoulder forward and the left hip forward, there will be a gentle twist to the body. Extend this to the next stride, where the left shoulder and the right hip are forward; the simple twist will be in the opposite direction. Extended through all the strides of a walking sequence, this action will represent a definite flexibility that would not normally appear in a walk action.

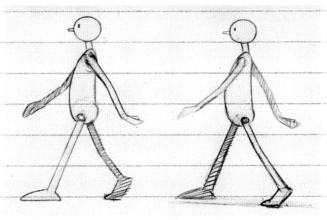

You can also gain great flexibility in your character by thinking about ways you can adapt even the most obvious of actions. For example, the legs in a simple walk action do not need to move forward and back in a conventional manner. Instead of bringing a leg through mechanically on a passing position, turn the knee out slightly as you bring it through and then in just before the foot hits the ground. This will give a fluid, quivery kind of action.

It is the same with the arms. Instead of moving them forward and back in a regular way on each stride, how about moving them like a bird flapping its wings, as I once did on the circular walk? It all brings a more fluid and flexible (if not a little eccentric) quality to the action.

One look at the great character animation of the past will reveal that even the fine traditional animators were aware of mass, volume, and anatomy. They also knew how to study these qualities in the real world and caricature them in the animated one. Look at the magnificence of Disney animation until and including the creation of *The Jungle Book*, especially the work of the greatest animators such as Frank Thomas, Ollie Johnson, and Milt Karl. Check out their pencil tests and see how flexible and three-dimensional their 2D character animation looked.

At the beginning of my career I would trace, frame by frame, the work of these greats to see exactly what they did and how they did it. It was only by stripping down Disney animation to the bare bones of pencil drawings that I could truly realize just how great that animation was. There is little to match it today, even with all the advanced technology and theories of process that abound.

I have featured this work before, but look at the recreated scene I once made for my film *Endangered Species*. I intently studied the animation of Pinocchio when he fell down the stage steps while singing "I've got no strings …" and then recreated it with my own character and my own background environment. I still don't believe I got half the way to the original greatness of that action, but it will at least allow me to illustrate the idea on the website without being sued for misuse of copyrighted material!

Squash and Stretch

Traditional flexibility in a character was always related to the principles of squash and stretch. Today, 2D and 3D animators tend not to rely on that traditional style of squash and stretch to express flexibility in a character, since contemporary animators tend to work with limbs, bones, and bodies of fixed length and mass. This is especially true in 3D animation, where character models are very much based on a fixed hierarchy of bones and joints. Old-fashioned "rubber hose" cartoon animators, however, always used a rubbery form of squash and stretch to express flexibility, and although it works perfectly well in that environment, it does seem a little out of place with modern approaches to animation.

Of course, this is not to say that the principles of squash and stretch should be ignored. They most definitely should not. However, unless a modern animator is deliberately going for a squashy cartoon effect or a rubber hose effect, the squash-and-stretch effect should be attempted when working with fixed anatomy rather than a rubbery anatomy. Consequently, a squash position should come from posing the character in a squashed shape, using bending arms in a fixed-length torso to produce the effect rather than physically squashing the anatomy unnaturally—unless the animation is meant to be in a "rubber hose" style that is!

Similarly, the stretch effect should be attempted by extending the physical qualities of the body anatomy as much as possible rather than stretching them abnormally, defying the principles of physics in the process.

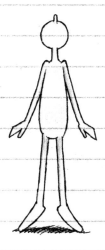

Secondary Bodily Movement

Remember, too, that if the limbs of the body move in some way, there will be some secondary action in the torso of the character at the same time. Consequently, if an arm is moved to the right from the left, there will be a slight sway to the body in that direction, too, probably pivoting from the waist—but possibly moving right down to the ankles. If a heavy object is being moved, the body will compensate for that by counterbalancing.

Also, if you are going to attempt something with great physicality, such as a spear throw, there has to be a marked element of flexibility in the action if it is to seem natural. Such an action will actually begin at the shoulder (and hence the body will motivate that), followed by the elbow and then by the wrist until the hand straightens out at the end of the action. Indeed, for complete flexibility and fluidity, the hand and arm might actually move beyond the end position and ease back into it with a slow-in. Again, there could be a slight bending of the wrist away from the final position as it does that.

Remember too that when animating anything, you are caricaturing real-life action, not duplicating it. Therefore, all movements have to be larger than life; the more cartoonish the animation needs to appear, the more that exaggeration process must be applied. The worst thing a traditional, hand-drawing animator can do is basically trace live-action movement in a rotoscope scenario, similar to a 3D animator using MoCap action to emulate real-life action. These techniques are often used for time and economy reasons, but left unmodified by an experienced animator, this action usually looks dead, wooden, or simply unnatural.

Also don't forget that all flexible motion will follow a path of action that is circular or arced rather than in a straight line. Think of our pitcher again. His movements might be huge or tiny, but they certainly are arced in action rather than straight.

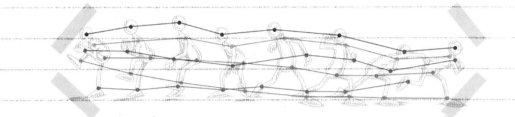

Face Flexibility

Of course, the face goes through an infinite range of fluid and flexible actions when a character is expressing herself. I will go into this concept in more depth in the next chapter on basic dialogue, but for now let's just discuss simple shape adjustments that will loosen up a character's performance. For example, simple surprise will have the face stretch longer.

This is not to say that we need to artificially extend the length of the face, but more that we move the existing anatomy of the face around to suggest that it is longer. Similarly, a character's reaction when she has seen something nasty happening will call for the face to squash up more. Again, though, this is not artificially squashing the face in any rubbery way, but within the physical nature of the facial geometry we can imply as much.

Don't forget that a character's eyebrows can do a lot to express emotion. Raised eyebrows will suggest surprise and amazement.

Downward-sloped eyebrows can suggest anger or confusion.

Turned-up eyebrows can suggest sadness or worry.

But again, unless the character is cartoony in nature, only work within the character's physical and anatomical limitations. Do not break the rules of "plausible implausibility."

Flexibility in Objects

So far we have discussed flexibility in characters, but quite often animation can be about moving graphic shapes and objects too. The principle of the bouncing ball is an obvious one.

However, there are others. For example, I have often used squash and stretch in animating hand-drawn lettering. This is something I once animated for a Scrabble commercial.

This was the start of bringing flexibility and fluidity to otherwise inanimate-looking text. See the website for another example of where the flexibility of the spider-like legs gives the animated lettering a really smooth quality.

I was once required to animate an orange doing a provocative, strip-tease dance. Today it would be done very realistically with CG technology, but in those days it had to be hand drawn, then pencil rendered, frame-by-frame, to look like a more realistic orange. The real success of the piece was the flexibility and fluidity of the peel as it came away from the fruit, especially at the very end.

Looking at some of the keyframes from the action, it is apparent that the use of arced convex and concave shapes within the peel drawings goes a long way to achieving the natural flexibility the whole piece contains.

It might help for me to explain something that can assist you in keeping the snap to shape changing in fluid animation. When we in-between from a concave shape to a convex one, it is tempting draw a straight breakdown drawing between them.

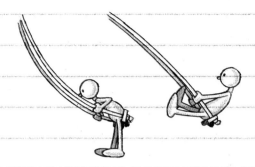

However, doing this only succeeds in making the overall action flatter than it need be. Consequently, it is strongly advised that a breakdown position between a concave and a convex shape should be close to a straight position but actually favor one of the two shapes a little.

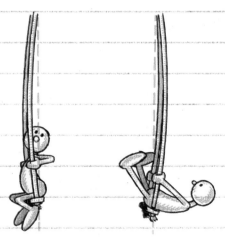

This provides a slight flip from one to the other rather than a logical, mechanical transition. This gives the snap that makes the animation look more vital and naturally energetic.

Suggested Assignment

Like a pianist who does extensive five-finger exercises before playing at a concert, it pays animators to limber up with a few exercises when they're learning to animate at a professional level. For fluidity and flexibility there are a couple of assignments you might consider doing to limber up. The first is to take a very simple object such as a pencil or a toothpick and have it bounce around and then do a flip. Look on the website at the pencil action I once animated for the *Endangered Species* crash scene.

Try to do the same yourself with a pencil or a toothpick and see how much natural fluidity you can get out of what on the surface appears as a solid object.

It you want to be a little more ambitious, consider taking a simple character and animating him conducting an orchestra. Ideally it would be good if you use music as your cue for the action, but you can do it mute if you like. The bottom line is that you need to show flexibility by having the character move his arms and baton in fluid, arced paths of action, using slow-ins and slow-outs to emphasize pace and timing. If you take this one on, though, I strongly suggest you work from reference footage of a real conductor, sketching out thumbnail key poses before attempting the full animation. That way you can push the dynamics of the key pose gestures without drawing in earnest. This helps capture a natural vitality of drawing that the full animation approach often inhibits. Remember, you are caricaturing real action, not emulating it!

chapter 12

Basic
Dialogue

**The animation of dialogue is a huge
subject and could take an entire book
to describe all aspects of its approach.
However, this chapter covers the core
basics that any animator should know
when animating a talking character.**

Dialogue is a special facet of animation that can take a lifetime
to learn in all its subtleties. Hopefully the following will give you
a solid foundation on which you can build your own knowledge
base of information.

As I indicated in *How to Make Animated Films*, the first thing we must accept about dialogue animation is the fact that it is not just about making the lips move in perfect synchronization with an audio track. Ultimately the lips do have to match the sounds they make, unless, of course, you are making anime, where it doesn't seem to matter! Effectively, for dialogue animation to make a real impact, the animator must first understand where the underlying emotion, expression, mood, and motivation are when words are being spoken, and then reflect that in the character's overall performance.

When it comes right down to it, it is the body language of the character that is more important than the accuracy of the lip movements. In fact, really good dialogue animation should be able to communicate the meaning of the words, even if the lips are not moving at all!

In live-action filmmaking, the lips tend to look like a blur—or at least a percentage of them look like blurs—whenever a character is talking. The faster the character talks, the more blurring there will be. This is because a single frame of film at 24 frames per second is not always fast enough to capture the rapid shape changes of the lips. We are more disadvantaged in animation, however, because whether we are producing traditional animation or CG-driven animation, we are forced to create hard-edged shapes for the mouths, giving a harder and more staccato look at times, which is still not fast enough to perfectly capture the changing mouth shapes.

The process and order of producing good dialogue animation can be suggested as follows: first, **body language**; second, **facial expression**; and third, **lip sync**. I tend to think that the body language provides the underpinning motivation or objective of what is being said, the facial expression communicates the emotion or mood of the speaker, and finally the lip sync is the technical connection between mouth shape and what is being spoken. I therefore approach this dialogue tutorial through these three crucial stages.

But First, Know Your Track!

Before we get into the nitty-gritty of dialogue performance, it has to be established that we can do nothing unless (and until) we have (and have understood) a strong audio dialogue track to which we need to animate. Usually the recording of the soundtrack will lie outside our involvement as production animators, so I focus more on the sound breakdown aspect of the audio process. A sound breakdown is a frame-by-frame analysis of the phonetic sounds that have been recorded during the audio capture. I have dealt with this topic more comprehensively in my book, *Animation from Pencils to Pixels*, so I will keep it very brief here.

Effectively, each frame of the dialogue sequence will need to be accurately analyzed and recorded before the animator starts. This way, the animator will know exactly what sound is heard on each frame of film he or she will be working with. Knowing this enables the animator to make sure that the right body language, facial expression, and lip sync shape will be presented for each frame of film to which they will be related.

ACTION	DIAL	EXTRA	4	3	2	1	EXTRA
001							
002							
003							
004							
005							
006	H						
007							
008							
009	O						
010							
011							
012	W						
013	T						
015	OO						
016	M						
017							
018	A						
019							
020	K						
021	E						
022							
023	N						
024							
025							
026	A						
027							
028	N						
029	I						
030							
031	M						
032	A						
033							
034							
035	T						
036	I						
037							
038	D						
039							
040							

Body Language

The first thing for an animator to do once the soundtrack has been recorded and broken down is to listen to it over and over again to get a strong sense of where the motivation and emphasis points are in the dialogue. Depending on what is being said, there will be key points in the delivery that give the animator clues as to what the character is saying, feeling, and expressing. These key points are moments that need to be emphasized in the action through pose and gesture.

So, once an animator has listened to the audio track enough times, he or she should start sketching out key pose thumbnail drawings that will define the character in the kinds of poses that the dialogue key points suggest. The secret is not to hold back at this stage. I continue to repeat, to the point of boredom, that the essence of great animation is the caricaturing of real life, not just imitating it. Therefore, your key poses can be extreme and exaggerated at this stage.

If you are lucky enough to have had the original recording material shot on videotape as the actor delivered the lines, you will get further clues as to how these thumbnail key poses should look. But this shouldn't preclude you from adding expression ideas of your own through the character's body language.

Rough Pose Test Animatic

What will help you most is to select your most favored key poses and shoot them as a key pose animatic. A key pose animatic basically enables you to shoot and time your key poses with the major soundtrack emphasis points synchronized to them. When you play this back, you will immediately get a sense of whether your thinking (and consequently the character's visual expression) is going the way you want it to.

Final Key Poses

When you are happy with the way your rough key pose animatic is going, you can begin to create your final key pose positions in the finished animation style of your choice. A traditional 2D animator will therefore draw up all his or her key pose drawings to style and with a continuity of character design throughout. These may not be the key cleaned-up drawings, of course, but they will be scaled to the correct style, and each drawing will be in size and shape continuity with the preceding and following keyframe drawings.

When these are done, you should again shoot a keyframe animatic to make sure all is working well in the finished animation style of your choice. If it is not, adjust as necessary, and then reshoot your key pose animatic.

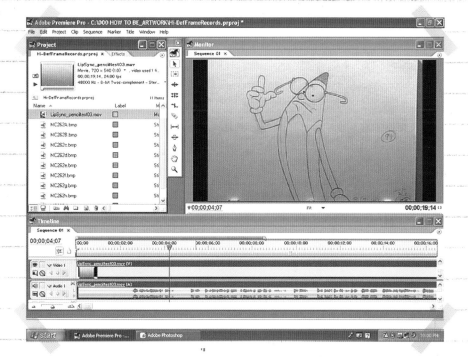

Tip

When timing out your keyframe drawings to a soundtrack, you will find that the visual/audio sync works better if you position each keyframe drawing several frames ahead of the actual sound to which you are attempting to sync it. For some reason this tends to appear more on-sync than if you time the keyframe exactly to the audio sound cues. If you do that, it will give the impression that the synchronization is late. (This also applies to open mouth positions when you're animating the mouth to strong vowel sounds. But we'll deal with that shortly.)

Facial Expression

With your keyframes in place to suggest the correct body language, it is time to add a little more emotion to the piece. Remember, the body language gives a hint of the motivation or intention of the dialogue being delivered, but the face will communicate the mood or the emotion behind the words. This expression of emotion is particularly focused around the eyes, but the overall facial positions can communicate a great deal of feeling, too.

It is estimated that there are something like 52 muscles in the human face, and each one of these muscles serves a purpose. The face therefore has a whole range of expressions outside the spoken word, so it pays to work hard at learning how you can communicate emotion just through the expressions you put in the face. Indeed, animators and/or character designers often create an "expression sheet" of the character to define this. As indicated, the actual shape of the mouth is secondary to this effort. It is what the face is saying, more than what the words are saying, that defines a great performance. To achieve a greater expression in the face, it is good to do a few exercises that will help your ability to deform a face to achieve certain results. A good way of doing this is the traditional bite 'n' chew exercise.

Bite 'N' Chew Exercise

Part of the great Disney internship program required student animators to successfully tackle the bite 'n' chew assignment.

Basically, students were requested to design a character holding a candy bar in his hand. The character would then be required to bring the bar to his mouth, showing a great deal of anticipation when he does so. This is followed up by the character biting a piece off the end of the candy bar and then chewing and swallowing it.

This entire exercise was designed to explore a full range of expressions in a character's face, in addition to learning snap, timing, and anticipation. All these elements are paramount for an animator drawing facial expression when attempting dialogue action.

Of course, students were not expected to simply imagine the bite 'n' chew action and animate it. They were required to act it out in a mirror for themselves and study every aspect of their facial expression throughout the action. They would be expected to repeat the exercise over and over again until they were able to produce a range of thumbnail keyframe drawings of the action before they attempted it in animation for real. Indeed, videotaping the action and playing it back again and again is an ideal way of approaching this process; doing so will give you unlimited time for study and analysis.

Things to be most aware of when researching this kind of exercise are the distortions in the face (but without distorting the essential skeletal structure beneath the face), the snap in timing when the end of the candy bar is bitten off, the circular, grinding chewing action on the jaw of the character, and the general expression of anticipation and fulfillment when the candy is being savored and swallowed. The way that the teeth grind and slide the candy in the mouth is an important aspect of the action, too.

Animating the Face

The bite 'n' chew exercise should give you a sense of how much the face can be pushed through a whole range of emotions and how it can be reasonably distorted to achieve mood or emotion. That is the purpose of the face in dialogue animation, so the sooner you learn to manipulate the face, the sooner your dialogue animation will begin to work well. Yet none of this can be achieved if you don't study the basics of facial expression first.

I always advise students who want to learn facial expression that they should first watch a great stage actor deliver a line of powerful dialogue. Even with TV soap operas we can see a certain range of cliché facial expressions that are cultivated to develop core moods and emotions.

The depth of subtle expression a good actor can achieve in a stage or film performance might not be possible in animation. But the finest animated dialogue can often achieve an acceptable range of core basic emotions. The look in the eyes, the appropriateness and timing of a blink, the hint and duration of a smile (or scorn), and the general presence of happiness, sadness, anger, and humiliation in the expression are all basic facial values that an audience will understand and appreciate. Remember, at this stage it has nothing to do with the shape of the mouths, it's just what the face is communicating as the words are heard.

So, when faced with a specific piece of dialogue, having drawn up all your key body poses first, go back and listen beyond the words and try to get a sense of the emotion they are seeking to express. Ask yourself, is the character angry, scared, witty, intellectual, seductive, or manipulative? Once you have decided the underlying motivation, you can begin to decide the kind of facial expressions you can apply to your character.

Again, if the recording session was captured on film or videotape, you can refer to that and see what the actor was actually doing with his face at the time of the recording. This will be a huge advantage. However, if this is not possible, listen to the words over and over, miming in a mirror and putting your own facial expressions to them. Study what your face is doing, and again, try to capture those actions with thumbnail key pose sketches.

If your dialogue has a happy quality to it, try to create happy expressions with your character's face. If there is anger, your character's face must express that emotion instead. Try to understand what particular emotion is driving your dialogue and devise your character's facial expressions accordingly. Sometimes a single line of dialogue can betray a whole range of expressions, so you need to capture these too, all in that one sentence.

The hardest expression to capture in animation is that subtle look that is often found in the eyes of great actors. In all forms of animation you have cruder means of achieving that same subtlety, but you must try.

For inspiration I always refer to the work of the great Disney animators of the distant past, such as master animators Frank Thomas and Ollie Johnson. Study what they did on *The Jungle Book, Lady and the Tramp*, and other such masterworks of animation, and you will appreciate what can be achieved at the highest level. (And only strive for the highest level you can, although I know it is desperately hard in this day and age to achieve anything near what they achieved.)

Yet excellence is possible if you're prepared to put in the hard work and right process. Again, I can only urge you to study intently the work of great actors as they deliver their lines. As with every other challenge in animation, if you can go to the closest source of reference for your material, you will be best informed.

That said, a few cliché tips might be useful. Remember that when the audience watches a speaking character on the screen, they will mostly focus on the eyes and not the mouth. So, when you are animating dialogue, make sure the eyes—and more specifically, the eyebrows—are delivering the emotional message that you want them to deliver. For example, a simple manipulation of the eyebrows alone can communicate some very basic emotion expressions.

For example, here's a neutral expression:

Angry:

Surprised or confused:

Worried:

Of course, these are approaches that are not particularly subtle. However, if you adapt them to the nature of your own character design, based on your observations of actors or your own interpretations in a mirror, you will begin to capture that special quality of eye expression that your dialogue needs.

Don't forget that a well-placed stare or blink can do wonders for punctuating the kind of emotion your dialogue action is trying to communicate.

Lip Sync

Finally, with motivation and emotion covered, it is time to approach the cherry on the cake, the lip sync.

Now we have to take special efforts to choose the correct shape of the mouth, the size of the mouth's opening, its timing, and its overall relationship to the expression and shape maintained by the face at any moment in time. This is easier said than done, especially, as with fast-talking dialogue, it is particularly difficult to fit every mouth shape that is necessary within the limitations of 24 frames per second. In such circumstances it is often necessary to choose between one particular mouth shape and another where two phonetic sounds straddle one frame of film. Consequently, animated lip sync can rarely be perfect, although with a slow-talking character it is often possible to achieve.

Having said all that, there are a number of key guidelines to lip sync that will help the decision-making process for every animator.

Vowel Sounds

Vowel sounds are the single most important element of lip syncing that has to be correct. Vowel sounds are the cornerstone of all lip sync mouth movement. The consonants are important, but not so important. The vowel sounds are a, e, i, o, and u aspects of work structure—basically, all the open-mouthed positions in speech.

Although there is a generic approach to all open-mouthed vowel sounds, the final shapes of the mouth have to be related into the nature of the character being animated. For example, a muttering, tight-lipped, poker player type of character will open his mouth in a far different way from a chatty, toothy, verbally dexterous TV chat show host. Again, it requires the animator to get beneath the skin of the character who is talking, and the character's mood and motivation, to interpret they way she will move her mouth.

Again, make good use of your mirror! Act out the lip sync and observe how your own mouth is working when you speak the words you are animating. Even if the natural look of your mouth is different from the shape of the character's mouth, try to emulate the basic shape of your character's mouth to see the shapes making the right words. Be the poker player! Be the toothy TV show host!

Vowel Anticipation

Just as I advised you to anticipate the sync frame with your poses on a key pose animatic, you should anticipate the open mouth positions on your vowel audio frames. As a general point I tend to advance the mouth positions around two or three frames ahead of their actual audio sync point, but sometimes with vowel sounds you can make it even more. As a general rule, the larger and more important the vowel sound, the more you might want to advance the open-mouth position. Bottom line: It is really a trial-and-error process, so it will help if you test various options on the most important ones as you attempt them.

This is also true for major other sync points such as coughs, sneezes, and explosive laughter. Some animators have actually anticipated these kinds of major impact points by anything up to 14 frames. But then again, testing through trial and error is the best way forward.

Tongue Action

The action of the tongue is a very important aspect of lip sync. If you watch yourself in a mirror as you speak dialogue, you will see how essential the tongue is, especially when the letter L is spoken. The tongue always goes to the top of the mouth whenever the letter L is pronounced. That said, unless your character's tongue is particularly active, try to keep it at the bottom of the mouth and as discreet as possible.

Note

You will find that if you hit the upward tongue action a couple of frames ahead of the actual L sound, it will always carry more impact.

Teeth

Not all animation characters have teeth, but the majority do. Consequently, if your character has teeth, remember that those teeth are fixed to the skull within the head. Consequently, never animate the teeth as though they are rubber or can move around in the head. Many animators have the teeth appearing sometimes and then not. Remember that the teeth are fixed somewhere behind the upper lip (depending on the design of the character's face), so you have to introduce them in a logical way—that is, only when the lips reveal them. To do anything else will be misleading and distracting.

Of course, if your character has buck teeth, you will be freer to introduce them more than at other times.

Some animators are "natural dialogue people" and others are not. So do not despair if your dialogue animation does not go well at first. Like most things, it's all a matter of trial and error—and ultimately experience. Dialogue animation requires fine-tuning and subtle expression. It also requires acute observation. Just as only a small percentage of actors are truly wonderful at Shakespeare, so too are some animators good at dialogue, whereas others are not.

But naturally good at it or not, always strive to be better at this process. The more you do it, the better you will be at it.

The important thing is to observe great actors as they work. They will offer you countless examples of how dialogue can be beautifully expressed, even with a minimum of movement. Look at video footage of actors as they deliver their lines. You will be amazed at the changes of their gestures and facial expressions, even on a frame-to-frame basis.

Above all else, listen to the audio track you have to animate and understand it on all its levels, whether the surface movement of the mouth shapes or deeper down, where motivation and emotion lie. Never forget that dialogue animation is not just about moving the mouth in perfect lip sync with the audio track—it is also about communicating the essence of the character that is speaking and why that character is saying the words it is saying.

Two-Character Dialogue

Finally, let's very briefly discuss two-character dialogue.

Two-character dialogue is not just about opposing characters looking at each other and talking. More often than not, dialogue between two characters involves a certain degree of intent—that is, one may be passive and one aggressive, one may be cruel and another a victim, one may be provocative and the other receptive. All these factors will affect the way you stage your scene and the way you handle your characters. Always remember that body language is everything.

Remember too that two-character animation is like a tennis match; one character is making the shot while the other one waits to receive it. Consequently, their stance, staging, and attitude should appear active and passive in a number of ways. Often a great truth can be communicated to an audience by focusing on the listener and not featuring the character that is speaking. By sharing the listening role among characters, the audience will often hear what is being said even more clearly.

Again, always test, correct, test, and correct your animation until everything is working well and as you want it.

Suggested Assignment

First and foremost, do the bite 'n' chew exercise because it will give you a sense of what you can do with a facially active character.

Second, go out into the community with a video camera and capture any real-life two-character dialogue interaction that you come across. Then select a suitable section of your movie (even a 5- or 10-second clip will work fine) and animate your own characters to match the words you've recorded. View the movie clip over and over again and analyze the subtleties of what you have on tape. Next plan your staging, thumbnail all the key poses for each of the speakers, and retranslate their gestures with your own character designs.

Remember

Make sure you caricature the action, and make sure your key poses are even more dynamic and expressive than the original action.

Animate as indicated in other parts of this book.

Index

Page numbers followed by *f* indicates a figure.